A Heart Like His

A Heart
Like His

*The Shaping of Character in
the Choices of Life*

REBECCA MANLEY PIPPERT

CROSSWAY BOOKS • WHEATON, ILLINOIS
A DIVISION OF GOOD NEWS PUBLISHERS

A Heart Like His

Published by Crossway Books
              a division of Good News Publishers
              1300 Crescent Street
              Wheaton, Illinois 60187

Edited by Kris Bearss, Lila Bishop, and Leonard G. Goss

Cover Design: Cindy Kiple

First printing, 1996

Printed in the United States of America

Library of Congress Cataloging-in-Publication Data
Pippert, Rebecca Manley.
    A heart like his : the shaping of character in the choices of life
    / Rebecca Manley Pippert.
        p.   cm.
    ISBN 0-89107-769-3
    1. Christian life.   2. Trust in God.   3. Witness bearing
(Christianity)   I. Title.
    BV4501.2P5544   1996
    248.4—dc20   96-18525

04		03		02		01		00		99		98		97		96
15	14	13	12	11	10	9	8	7	6	5	4	3	2	1

To my children,
Elizabeth and David

With love, joy, and my heartfelt prayer
That you will grow up to be
a woman and a man after God's own heart

CONTENTS

Preface / ix

Introduction: The Making of a Heart / 13

1 FEAR: *A Miserable Way to Live* / 27

2 FAITH: *The Remedy for Fear* / 43

3 ENVY: *A Sure Road to Self-Destruction* / 59

4 COMPASSION: *The Remedy for Envy* / 81

5 HATRED: *A Consuming Fire* / 93

6 LOVE: *The Remedy for Hate* / 115

7 REBELLION: *When the Heart Turns Hard* / 129

8 SUBMISSION: *The Remedy for Rebellion* / 145

9 ANGER: *A Force That Must Be Reckoned With* / 163

10 MEEKNESS: *The Remedy for Anger* / 181

11 DESPAIR: *A Turning Point, or the End of the Line?* / 195

12 HOPE: *The Remedy for Despair* / 209

Conclusion / 227

PREFACE

For as long as I can remember, I have been deeply drawn to the biblical person of David. His passionate love for God, earthy spirituality, and uncompromising humanity speaks to me, as it has to believers throughout the centuries. David lives the complexities, ambiguities, and struggles of human life with a sensitivity and depth and openness rarely seen in our superficial age of formula answers.

But more than this, David knows what to do with all of his humanity—he brings it to God! David brings his scars, wounds, failures, and petitions to the One who knows us, the One from whom "no secret can be hid." He is a God who can be trusted for every season of our lives. David never doubts God's overriding sovereignty. Because David understands that the issue in life is not whether God will be faithful to us, but whether *we* will be faithful to God.

I was drawn once again to reread the book of Samuel during a very difficult and painful time in my life. As I read the narrative and spent time in the Psalms, I found that David gave voice to the entire range of human experience. He prayed with raw honesty, and he came to God empty-handed, offering nothing but his desperate faith. But through the process, God strengthened his faith, deepened his character, and transformed David's pain into praise. We see that no part of our humanity is alien to God's saving work in our lives.

I was asked to lead a Bible study for women in the Washington, D.C., area using Diana Schick's wonderful materials from the *Creative Living* Bible studies. I was told that the women didn't want "fluff" or "niceness." They wanted real answers that dealt with the real problems of life. *Whom better to turn to than David,* I thought?

When I saw firsthand how powerfully David communicated to both seekers and believers alike, it convinced me that all of us deep down are thirsting for real answers. Saccharine and superficial solutions will not do. The solutions must realistically address the profound problems of life. But beyond the pain and complexity of our lives, we long for God to make a deep and joyful difference. I believe the story of David does just that by teaching us how to become whole and truly human in God.

There is much discussion today about the crisis of character and what it means to be authentically human. As I studied the book of Samuel, I was intrigued by how the development of vital faith impacts the formation of our character and how frequently God uses adversity as the catalyst to develop our character.

I do not take the classical approach of examining the seven deadly sins or the seven virtues. Instead I try to follow the contours of the narrative and let the text lead us, on its own terms, into a discussion of the virtues. Since the book of Samuel is such an unlaundered history, with its passionate commitment and concern for realism, we don't have to read very far before we see that it's all there—the surprises and seductions, the ambiguities and power struggles, the mixed motivations and incongruities that make up human life. But what is also revealed are the gifts, grace, wisdom, faithfulness, and presence of God.

I truly take great pleasure in expressing gratitude to the many persons whose contributions to this book, be it in the form of insights, loving friendship, or prayers, have inspired, encouraged, and corrected me at many points. I especially want to thank my friends who deserve my warm and deepest gratitude for having encouraged me throughout the process of writing. These include Fred and Elizabeth Catherwood, David and Felicity Bentley-Taylor, David and Pamella

Boch, Billy and Nancy Gray, Eugene and Jan Petersen, Thena Ayers, Clark and Beverly Parsons, Paul and Virginia Friesen, Doug and Adele Calhoon, Sid and Jane Anderson, Ben and Lauretta Patterson, Herman and Sue Kanis, Leanne Payne, Ethel Renwick, Jim and Ruth Nyquist, and Arloween. Special thanks for the kindness and enormous generosity of Sally and Kristina Nevius and Bob and Martha Molenhouse. Also warm thanks to my daughter's third grade class, when she attended Rosepark Christian School, who prayed weekly for me.

I am very grateful to my friend Dr. Os Guinness and the Trinity Forum for making their insightful curriculum papers available for public use and for providing me with several quotations. I also thank Rev. Timothy Brown for the opportunity to preach and teach and lead a study on the book of Samuel while I was at Christ Memorial Church in Holland, Michigan. And I especially thank him for being so gracious and understanding when I asked for a leave of absence to focus my full attention on the book. I am also indebted to my friend, Dr. Carol Simons, philosophy professor at Hope College, for her help and insights regarding the classical moralists.

To my editor Len Goss, I want to express warm thanks and deep gratitude for your help, encouragement, and support, and to all of the staff at Crossway my thankfulness for your Job-like patience!

Finally, very special thanks goes to my family. To my dear father and mother, to Bob and Cathy, I love you.

Most of all I want to thank my precious children to whom this book is dedicated. Elizabeth and David have supported me so much through the process of writing. They celebrate its completion with me, and together we offer it to you, the reader, with gladness and praise to God.

INTRODUCTION:
THE MAKING OF A HEART

L ife. It is much worse than I ever imagined and far better than I could have dreamed. No one is exempt from life's pain or God's blessings.

Yet in the midst of tragedy and triumph, there is something I find strangely heartening: sin never changes. We may dress it up and call it by different names—disorder, dysfunction, addiction—but the traps and temptations have not changed very much. Neither have we. Whether we admit it or not, all of us are engaged to one degree or another in a personal, ongoing battle with sin. Believer or atheist, moral philosopher or criminal, beloved minister or rapist—in the end, all of us are flawed human beings who must grapple with our own inner natures.

That is not to minimize sin's horror and potential for damage. But for all the pain that sin produces, at its core it is downright boring. There is nothing "original" about sin—it's all been done before. The only real surprise in life is God, who continually amazes us with the unexpected. And that is heartening.

Why is God such a surprise? Well, how would *you* like to deal with flawed, rebellious earthlings from time immemorial? If God were like us, wouldn't he be saying by now, "If I have to hear *one* more problem, *one* more excuse, I think I will lose my cosmic mind!

I've given them everything they need to guide them to truth and wholeness, but they still don't get it. I need a vacation!"

But God is not like us. The Bible reveals a God who is loving, holy, and merciful, who opens his arms to us and who is constantly seeking the attention of his sinful children. He promises that he can take whatever we give him—all that is flawed and broken and wrong—and create something new and beautiful. He delights to bring mercy and grace in the most unexpected and creative ways. He brings hope out of despair, healing out of brokenness, and new life out of barrenness. Not overnight, but slowly and surely.

The good news is that while life is difficult and sin an ever-present reality, God offers hope and healing for all who need it. The bad news is that we *all* need it! The only way we differ is that some of us realize our need, and some do not.

What is it then that blocks us from seeing the truth about our own nature and God's nature? There are many answers to this question— pride being at the top of the list. But I want to suggest another factor of particular relevance today. Live though we may in this fast-paced, fact-swirling information age, we still know less about the issues that matter most than our ancestors did. We belong to an age that is as con- fused about God's nature as it is about human nature.

First, our view of God is shortsighted. Too often we see God as a celestial Santa Claus who is far too enlightened to be bothered with such antiquated nonsense as "who has been naughty or nice." He just wants to fill our stockings with the toys of our choice. Or we have the opposite problem. We see God as a celestial Scrooge who wants our lives to be dreary, drab, and dull. The truth is, it's the other way around. The Bible shows us that it is *God* who grieves the most when we miss out on the joy, the peace, and the ecstasy that he intends for us. As C. S. Lewis said in *The Weight of Glory,* " . . . it would seem that Our Lord finds our desires, not too strong, but too weak. We are half-hearted creatures, fooling around with drink and sex and ambi- tion when infinite joy is offered us, like an ignorant child who wants to go on making mud pies in a slum because he cannot imagine what is meant by the offer of a holiday at the sea. We are far too easily pleased."

All around me I see people who are weary and disgusted with their mud pies. They would love nothing more than to enjoy the peaceful, restorative refreshment of the sea. But they don't know how to get there. They don't even know what to pack for the journey or what to leave behind.

Second, we don't believe that God intends for us to be truly human. We think we must get dressed up in our Sunday best to talk to God. We're afraid that being made of flesh and blood meets with divine disapproval. The fact that we love to laugh, sip tea with a friend, play tennis with a passion, or read a book for the sheer pleasure of it is probably regarded from on High, we fear, as: "Oh, all right. Do it if you *must*." We forget that it was God's idea, not ours, to make us human. But God did not fashion us as angels who operate only in the realm of the spirit, nor did he make us as animals without will or reason. God made us *human*. Yet we fear that somehow our very humanness is unacceptable to God.

Third, because we don't understand God's nature or his purposes for us, we may be the most confused about what it means to be authentically human. We tend to cling to our old religious stereotypes—that to be a devout person necessitates being dour, fearful lest we make a mistake, careful not to have too much fun, and cautious to appear perfect. Surprisingly, the biblical view is that we only become truly ourselves, and most authentically human, when we live and walk before God in complete transparency, intimacy, passionate love, and unapologetic dependence upon him.

God does not want to deprive us of our humanity. On the contrary, he wants us to understand what enhances our humanity and what destroys it. The Bible says that sin—or vice—distorts and debases our humanness but that virtue heightens it.

So to live life on one's toes, with maturity and skill, we must possess at least three things: (1) *faith* in God, for it enables us to find our true self, the self God created us to be, (2) *moral knowledge*, for it helps us understand what destroys our humanity and what enhances it, (3) *the power of God's Spirit,* for it is through the Spirit's power (and our obedience) that we are able to walk victoriously.

Recognition of the need for faith, moral knowledge, and the Spirit's power, while not a new insight, seems all but forgotten in modern times. Why is this? Because in modern cultures people no longer perceive reality as centered in God, the One who completes and fulfills us. Today the real "I AM" is "me." Faith in God ranks way below the ultimate modern goal: having faith in ourselves!

I went to a lecture given by a very successful entrepreneur. She began her lecture by asking the crowd, most of whom were Christian businessmen and women: "How many of you believe in yourselves 100 percent?" No hands were raised. "Okay, then how many of you believe in yourselves 95 percent? Or 90 percent?" Someone foolishly raised his hand.

Then she asked, "Where did Jesus' success come from? It came from believing in himself *100 percent*—and so must you! Ninety-five percent is not good enough! Follow Jesus' example and believe in yourself 100 percent."

I watched in astonishment as the crowd applauded enthusiastically. I raised my hand and said, "Excuse me, but do you really think Jesus spent his time on earth trying to convince people to believe in *themselves?* Wasn't he rather trying to help people believe in his Father in heaven? I'm sure Jesus was self-confident. But then if I were God, I'd be a lot more self-confident too! I'd worry about a God who had to take self-esteem courses on the side. However, didn't Jesus try to help us see that our essential humanity is useless? Isn't our problem today that we believe in ourselves *too much?* I fear you are taking away the very thing that brings us to the truth and enables us to see our need for God—the realization of our inadequacy."

"Now isn't that a helpful insight?!" the lecturer said. "That's why we need discussions like this. So that we can see that no statement is right or wrong; they all lead us to God." Her response was indicative of another problem we have in modern culture—the loss of absolute truth. Without a clear understanding of God, who is truth, we lose our confidence in objective truth and objective moral law. The sad fact is, few people today believe that there are external moral laws that govern life.

That fact came home to me recently when I was invited to give a talk on the topic of vice and virtue. A woman in the audience objected strongly when I said that vices such as pride or envy debase and destroy our humanity, whereas virtues like compassion and humility strengthen us and make us better.

"But don't you see?" she exclaimed with a look of horror. "By saying this you are suggesting that some things are wrong and other things are right. Personally, I *prefer* to be compassionate, but I don't think I should impose that on someone else."

"I see. Then according to your approach, it's fine if I prefer pepperoni on my pizza, just as I prefer not to engage in child abuse, because it's my choice. But, hey, if someone else prefers sausage and abuse, then that's fine too?"

She answered, "I don't think child abuse is correct under any circumstances, but we must be very careful not to be intolerant."

"But you *are* intolerant of abuse, and you just said so. Why do you resist acknowledging some things as right or wrong when in your deepest heart you know they are?"

"Because I have been taught that to be a thinking person, I must be open-minded!" she snapped back.

"Well," I responded, "as one of my favorite graduate professors used to say, 'The trouble with being *too* open-minded is that your brains fall out.'"

We live in an age in which it appears that our brains truly have fallen out—if having an "enlightened intolerance" of the things that destroy us is dismissed as being narrow-minded and prudish. I left that lecture shaking my head in disbelief at how far our modern mind-set has drifted from what our ancestors took for granted.

Our ancestors believed in moral categories. They wrestled deeply over what constituted good and bad character. They understood the conflict between temptation and virtue. They took seriously the horrible effect that pride, envy, hate, anger, greed and lust have on our character. They saw vice as truly deadly. They also believed that as we develop virtues such as love, temperance, humility, and compassion, we become more whole as humans.

But in modern times, with the loss of objective truth and objective moral law, we are reduced to conduct that is informed not by principles but by personal preference. The vice and virtue tradition that once contributed to the western definition of humanness does so no longer. Today, we minimize and scoff at any notion of sin, and we regard virtue as pietistic, moralizing nonsense that prevents us from being free. Never mind that every conceivable vice is represented by an association of devotees today. Thieves, gluttons, lechers, the violent, those consumed by envy or despair—they all have their own meetings to attend that center around their failure to master their physical and psychological impulses. I am not demeaning the value of these groups. I am only pointing out the irony that our "freedom" from believing in sin has produced "Anonymous" clubs that absolutely verify sin's existence.

The problem in modern western civilization is not that we are more susceptible to sin than our ancestors were, but that we know so much less about moral truth and our need for absolutes. The difference is not in our *natures* but in our *knowledge*. Our modern problem is that to practice morality, we must first know what it is. We can't attain what we do not understand. Our ancestors understood that their problem was not living up to their principles. Our problem is not having any principles. In *The Abolition of Man*, C. S. Lewis described the difference this way: "For the wise men of old, the cardinal problem of human life was how to conform the soul to objective reality, and the solution was wisdom, self-discipline and virtue. For the modern, the cardinal problem is how to conform reality to the wishes of man, and the solution is the technique."

The fact that most moderns seem to be uninformed about thousands of years of moral tradition in literature forces us to ask another vital question: How do we educate our children without a foundation in moral knowledge? As ethicist Christina Sommers said in an interview with *Christianity Today:* "We may well be the first society in history that finds itself hamstrung in the vital task of passing on its moral tradition."

A few years ago, I served as a classroom teacher's aide once a week for the first three years that my children attended public school. The children were delightful, enthusiastic, and curious. But I was surprised to see how they interpreted the meaning of the stories during story hour. The same themes kept recurring in their comments: "I'm entitled." "It's my right." "It's okay if it makes you happy, if you don't hurt anyone, or if you don't get caught." The children certainly could not have articulated their position philosophically, but it slowly dawned on me that I was dealing with seven-year-old moral agnostics. And no behavior motto over the door could possibly overcome the cultural assumption that most of these children unconsciously carried with them as they walked through the door.

I shared some of these observations recently in a conference of Christians. One man in the audience said, "Yes, but the world will always be in crisis without knowing God and following his ways. The solution lies in living before them the difference that Christ makes."

"I couldn't agree more," I responded. "But at the same time, I must ask: Are we truly living that difference? Would the world affirm that one of our distinguishing characteristics is that we can look honestly at ourselves and our own flaws? Would skeptics look at us and conclude, especially by the way we love and show mercy, that we are people after God's own heart? I want to believe so, but I'm not sure."

Recently many Christian colleges across America have reported a remarkable movement of God's Spirit on campus. Hundreds of students spontaneously confessed sin and repented of former lifestyles. This is cause for great rejoicing. Yet, we must ask, why was there such a discrepancy between students' beliefs and behavior? During this revival, many Christian colleges reported confessions of rape, homosexual affairs, drug and alcohol abuse, promiscuity, and cheating on exams. At one, after a deeply moving service of repentance, someone brought in five large garbage bags and asked students to throw away whatever represented their old life. All five bags were filled to the rim. A consistent concern was voiced by many of the students: "Now that I've emptied myself of sin, how do I keep from going back to it? What do I put in its place?" And most heartbreaking of all: "How can I be of any use to God when I feel like such damaged goods?"

I heard many faculty and administrators say that they knew how to help the students turn from what was destroying them. But when it came to teaching them how to develop Christian virtues, or instructing them in how to walk in the power of the Holy Spirit, they were not sure they had mastered that themselves.

We may say that those are just the temptations of youth and that "they'll grow out of it." Yet how often have we seen more seasoned Christians who accept the biblical rule yet who live in ways that violate what they say they believe? Their sins aren't perhaps the sins of the flesh, as with the young, but their sins, according to the Bible, are even worse. They are the sins of the spirit—pride, envy, and hate. They are the sins that lead to a judgmental, critical attitude toward others, usually resulting in gossip and slander. How often have we seen the young turn away from God because of the harshness and unloving behavior demonstrated by those they considered mature in faith?

We must admit it: there is a schism between what we say we believe and how we live. There is a failure—both in the church and in the world—to live up to what we know to be true (for even skeptics will admit in a candid moment that they know they should behave better than they do).

Once we acknowledge how radical the problem is, then we can begin to see that there is indeed an answer. Then we are ready to discover the hope that only God can give—to realize that he has provided all the resources and models we will ever need to live in a way that is all at once glorifying to God, deeply human, and overflowing with the joy of life. That doesn't mean God gives us an immunity shot to keep away life's difficulties. Rather he promises his strength and grace to overcome the trials.

When it comes to the question of how God breaks us and shapes us and makes us into the people he would have us become, there is no story in God's Word, let alone in the rest of written literature, that shows us more clearly than that of David, King of Israel.

At first glance, the story of David seems to be anything but a morality tale. We see human cunning and pathology. We see people lie, envy, hate, murder. But we also see what happens when people open themselves and respond to God, and how their moral character is formed and shaped over time.

Ancient though David's story may be, we share many of the same problems he had. Israel, though instructed by her founding fathers in the ways of God and in the reality of moral absolutes, was drifting away from her roots. Israel was in fact in moral chaos and increasingly open to religious idolatry. Politically, the nation was weak and in short supply of true leaders. Culturally, the people were in crisis. What did God do to help? He sent individuals who modeled for their time and for all time how we can become God's people in the midst of very difficult circumstances.

Three men dominate this narrative in First and Second Samuel: Samuel the prophet, Saul the king, and David, the man who would become the greatest king Israel had ever known. It is through David, however, that our most powerful instruction will come.

We know more about David than almost any other person in the Bible. Besides being an exemplary ruler, he was a military and political genius, a poet of exceptional skill, a talented musician, and the architect who designed the temple that his son Solomon built. Usually a person that gifted intimidates us. Yet people genuinely loved and were drawn to David.

Why is he still so appealing even thousands of years later? I asked a friend what came to her mind when she thought of the biblical David. "Human!" she answered in a flash. Her answer was on target. Larger-than-life, passionate, and gifted though David was, what draws us to him was his humanity. As we read his psalms, we realize that he not only understood our feelings but that he shared them. As we read the central events of his life—the progression from shepherd boy to king of Israel—we feel he was one of us.

Why? Because David was so real. He was unapologetically human. Religious people are often stereotyped as unassertive and anemic. But David, who worshiped God with every fiber of his being, was bursting with life and vitality! He loved God, and he loved people. He openly admitted his faults. When tragedy occurred, and it looked as if David and his men would never see their loved ones again, David did not plaster on a saccharine smile and lead his men in a rousing chorus of "People Need the Lord." Instead, he wept until he could weep no more, and then he "strengthened himself in the Lord." David danced; he cried; he made mistakes; he had trouble with his kids; he expressed his pain, his fear, his confusion, and anger with raw honesty to God.

How we need David's example of earthy spirituality! His humanity *strengthened* his faith and made it easier to trust God. And as he trusted God, he became more like God.

And what is God's verdict on such a passionate expression of humanity? God *liked* it. God did not say, "David, could you just tone it down a bit? Your dancing might be a real stumbling block to your followers. Couldn't you be a little less exuberant and act more *religious?*" Instead, the Lord said in effect, "Now there's a man after my own heart."

David's faith in God was deep and sparkling, his reverence for the truth of God's laws, profound. Yet he was also deeply flawed. His sins were usually as visible as his gifts. Sometimes he was consumed by ambition and revenge. On one occasion, he committed a murder that was a deliberate and determined evil. He was capable of most sins and culpable of many. He gave in to sudden and dangerous passion, and he always suffered the consequences. But we never see him trying to be more or less than a human being before God. He pulled no punches about life's difficulties. He wrestled with fear and hope, confusion and faith, horror at his own sin, as we see in the psalms. But he always faced his sin, repented from the heart, and came back to the God he served and loved with all his soul. He did all this openly before God. Indeed, David was open and human as few leaders in history have ever been.

Like many of us, David was wounded emotionally. His origins weren't easy. He was left alone a great deal as a child, and sometimes his family did not treat him lovingly. When he was insulted, he overreacted. That makes us wonder if the insult turned a knife in a deep wound. The benefit of David's pain was that the world never satisfied his needs. But God did. God saw that lonely, love-starved shepherd boy with the poetic imagination and set out to shape him into the man he envisioned David to be.

It was hard work because the future king was both wounded and sinful. But David's heart responded to God's love with deep fervor. He loved God above all else. That is why David's story speaks to us. It invites all of us, the wounded, broken, and suffering—the sinners, as well as those who have been deeply sinned against—are invited to come and listen to his story, to discover fresh hope. If David were here to speak to us today, he would no doubt say, "God never gave up on me until he had accomplished what he had started. He will never give up on you either."

How could David speak with such assurance? Because he went through a "wilderness season" both literally and figuratively. These were the years when David lived as a fugitive pursued by King Saul, and they were truly the making of the man. When he finally became king, David would draw on all of the character lessons he had learned in those very difficult years, and those lessons would guide him to obedience and faith.

We will look especially at David's time in the wilderness, as well as the events that immediately precipitated his departure from Saul's court, as the background to our discussion for this book. This narrative teaches us so much on so many different levels. One level concerns Israel's radical political transition from a theocracy (where God was king) to a monarchy (where a human king governed in submission to God). During this transformation, Israel ceased to be a marginal company of unstable tribes and became a powerful centralized state.

On another level, the text addresses the importance of faith in the development of our character. The story is full of life, pathos, and power. It shows rather than tells the evil of sin and the goodness of faith and virtue. We will study those vices and virtues as revealed through the fascinating characters of David and Saul. Vices such as fear, envy, hate, rebellion, anger, despair, and pride. And virtues such as faith, compassion, love, obedience, meekness, hope, and humility.

Maybe you are going through some wilderness time of your own. You have wondered how or even if you will get through it. You wonder if there is someone who understands the difficulties and complexities of life, someone who has faced the same doubts, dismay, anger, and pain. You know you need someone who can identify with your suffering. But more than that, you need someone who can show you how your wilderness experience can lead to deeper faith and strength. You long for someone who has been completely honest about his own trials and yet who has come out on the other side of them to tell you that God is good and that he is trustworthy. That we are not left alone in the universe to fend for ourselves. That God truly is there. That he not only sustains us in our suffering, but he will use the pain to make us better than we ever were.

If you are still looking for an example to follow, then David is your man. Through David we see what adversity can produce in a person's life when that person is walking with God. David clung to God and related to him with intimacy and passion, showing us what a true relationship with God could be like. It is a relationship of heart and soul right in the midst of the traumas of everyday life. Everything David thought, felt, delighted in, or regretted was viewed in relationship to this living God. David's relationship to God was one of such delight and awe that it is impossible to understand the man unless you know his God. David's life makes no sense apart from God. David lived like a man who knew that God is real, which is why he was always praying. He felt free to voice his doubts and confusion because he knew that either God is everything, or he is nothing. David knew that the only thing he absolutely needed was the only thing he was absolutely guaranteed: God.

In the final analysis, the most basic problem we all have is a problem of the heart. Not in a sentimental, romantic sense. Not even in a pious, religious sense. But a problem of the heart in the biblical sense, where we find the wellspring of life—the center of the human spirit, the source of our emotions, thoughts, will, courage, and actions. What we need is a heart like David's that cries out passionately to God to "create in me a clean heart." More than this, we need "a heart like his"—a heart that draws its life moment by moment from the living God, our Creator and Redeemer.

In the life of David we see the answer—how God used the choices and crises of David's life to transform his character and shape him into the person God would have him be. The good news is that God will do the same in our lives—if we are willing to let him. It is my hope that as we encounter David in the following chapters, we will come face to face with this extraordinary man from the Bible and that in doing so, we will come face to face with who *we* are. But more than anything, I hope that we would encounter the living God and by his grace be transformed into the people he would have us to be—people with hearts like his.

Chapter
One

Fear:
A Miserable Way to Live

A friend of mine called recently. I could tell by the sound of her voice that something was very wrong. "The diagnosis is cancer, and the operation is in two weeks," she confided. She is a strong woman with a vibrant faith in Christ, but as I listened to her struggling to process the news, one question kept emerging. "I know this may sound funny, but I don't know how to *think*. I've read books telling me it's possible to heal yourself of cancer through proper nutrition, a healthy lifestyle, and building up my immune system. Then I've read books that some consider a faith approach that say to pray and claim victory over the cancer. But I think both approaches are afraid to admit the obvious, that some things are beyond our ability to control. I do pray and I've always been committed to a healthy lifestyle, but that doesn't insure that the cancer will go away. I almost get the feeling from these books that if I die it's my fault, because I didn't eat that one particular food or pray that one particular prayer that could have conquered the cancer.

"Becky, the bottom line is that I'm scared. I don't want to die. Does my fear mean that I don't trust God as I thought I did? How can I *not* be afraid of a deadly disease? How do I deal with my fear, trust God and find courage?"

Another friend, an eminent surgeon, told me that she is being sued for malpractice. She is a wonderful surgeon, conscientious and cautious. She cares deeply for her patients. She feels the suit is unfair, and she hopes to win the case. But the issues she wrestles with are similar to those of my friend with cancer. "If I lose this case, it's not only my professional reputation that is on the line. It could be my life savings too. How do I deal with the dread that wakes me up in the middle of the night? It would be foolhardy not to be alarmed. But the truth is, there is so little I can control, other than being sure I am well-prepared for the trial. It feels as if my future rests in the hands of an unknown jury and unnamed judge. I remind myself that God is sovereign, but what exactly does that mean? Do I tell myself I have nothing to fear because God is faithful? Does trusting God mean I should assume that justice will be done?"

There is no emotion quite so debilitating as fear. One minute we are reasonably confident and on top of things, and the next minute we get blindsided. We go from feeling that life is fairly under control to feeling that even the ground we walk on is not as secure as before. Fear taps into our deepest anxieties, and into those areas over which we have little control—our health, our children's destinies, our reputation, our financial or professional success.

But as immobilizing as fear can be, it brings us a vital lesson if we are honest: it reminds us that we are inadequate. Life, in fact, *is* too much for us. Sooner or later we will all face a situation that leaves us sobered by our inadequacy. We become aware that our gifts, knowledge, character and expertise are no guarantee of success. That is not negative thinking. It is simply seeing things realistically. When the odds are truly against us and we are not a little bit afraid, it implies that we simply don't know what is going on.

Why is seeing our inadequacy helpful? Doesn't such an admission intensify the very fear we are trying to overcome?

The silver lining in the dark cloud of fear is that fear pushes us to decide on our view of reality. What do I truly believe about the universe? Am I alone in this battle, or is there a God who overrules human affairs? Does my deliverance depend upon human prowess and things

I can see, or does the final outcome depend on a massive resource beyond my own—the powerful, faithful, living God?

If God is real then it's *God*-confidence we need far more than self-confidence. Furthermore, if there is a God, then the only correct way to perceive reality is through faith in him. Evil may seem to be winning the day, but appearance ultimately does not count for much, because God is always sovereignly involved.

How then does faith in God's sovereignty determine the way we handle fear? How can we trust the unseen reality of God when what we *can* see terrifies us? These are the very issues with which our story begins.

NO CONTEST: DAVID AND GOLIATH (1 SAMUEL 17)

Saul was immobilized by fear. He had been listening to Goliath make rude and threatening comments about Israel and Israel's God day in and day out, and his failure of faith had paralyzed the entire army. No doubt Saul would say in his defense, "Hey! Look at what I was up against!" The biblical narrator agreed, and paid enormous attention to the physical attributes of Goliath, including his height and his armor. His awesome size was matched only by his bombastic style, a style that exuded total self-confidence. He was the worst kind of bully there is: an armed-to-the-teeth kind.

Israel was intimidated and terrified, and so was Saul. No one knew what to do. Goliath's sword was larger and longer than anyone else's. There would be no contest in a battle between weapons—they knew it and so did Goliath. Maybe Goliath did not have "the whole armor of God," but he sure had the whole armor of man.

Who was going to save the day? The only One who ever can. It is God who is the real rescuer in life's traumas.

But God prefers some raw material to work with. Who then? A governor with political clout? A military captain with a larger army? No, a shepherd boy with the menial task of carrying the lunch boxes to and fro! A kid who was not only considered too young to fight in the battle, but who had the dubious distinction of being the eighth, and hence powerless, son in a seemingly unimportant family within a seem-ingly insignificant tribe.

Previously, the Lord had warned the prophet Samuel not to look at appearances, because what matters to God is one's heart. Who had the right stuff? Enter David: the boy whose only qualification was that he had the kind of heart that God values. And that, as it turned out, was everything.

As insignificant as David may have seemed outwardly, from the moment he stepped on the scene we sense the vitality of his person. David arrived in camp just as a battle was getting under way. He was so eager to see what was going on that he left the supplies and ran to the front lines, arriving just in time to hear Goliath's taunt: "I defy the armies of Israel this day; give me a man that we may fight together." The army of Israel was so terrified by Goliath's threats that they imme-diately scattered and fled. But David was not afraid. In fact, he was fascinated and clearly intrigued by what he understood would be the consequences of defeating Goliath.

Far more importantly, David heard in Goliath's taunts what appar-ently no one else did. Saul and his army were so focused on Goliath's vicious words and intimidating bravado that they missed the main point! But after listening for only a few seconds to the giant's threats, David innocently asked, in so many words, the question that no one else thought to ask: "Ah, excuse me, but did you happen to catch what that guy just said? He has just defied the living God. Nobody can get away with that and live!"

Now this is a particularly embarrassing point. For starters, Goliath had been doing this for forty days, and there is no record that Saul or anyone else in the army had even mentioned God before. But this was practically David's first thought! *Indeed, Saul had behaved as if God was irrelevant to the battle.*

If God was irrelevant in this battle, then Israel was in deep trou-ble. They were no match for the Philistines in terms of weaponry or military training. But David did not believe that God was irrelevant. Indeed, for David it was unthinkable to assess anything in life apart from the rule of the living God.

The innocent question really was a reprimand: Is there a God or not? Is there a divine power intimately concerned with life's battles and sordid affairs? Does God make a difference in our present danger, or does he watch from a remote distance? One need only experience real fear once to know that it matters desperately whether there is a divine power outside of ourselves that can neutralize and overcome any present danger.

How we see reality matters a great deal. Whose definition of reality would prevail was the core issue between David and Saul, as well as between David and Goliath.

Because David's response to the situation was so markedly different from everyone else's, he was immediately ushered in to see Saul. He spoke boldly of his experience and qualifications. His argument was, "I've been in dangerous situations before, so you can trust me."

Saul was desperate. Yet even in his state of troubled terror he could not imagine how an innocent-looking boy could possibly fight against the fierce and terrifying Goliath. After all, this was the real world—a world in which grown-ups have enormous responsibilities, with life-and-death consequences. He must have sighed wistfully as he saw young David, so bold and sure! Oh, to be that confident!

But David continued undeterred. Furthermore, he argued, it was not his prowess or courage that helped him but "the Lord." "The Lord who delivered me from the paw of the lion and from the paw of the bear, will deliver me from this Philistine." For the first time in Saul's presence David made a theological argument.

Now we see why David's courage had not melted. It was because he did not abandon God, his only source of hope.

David had a different perception of the battle because he saw it as theologically rooted. As far as David was concerned, life's difficulties always present us with a choice. Do we trust in appearances or in the unseen living God? For David there was no contest, because he was convinced that beyond appearances lay the deeper reality of God.

Saul was persuaded. But Saul, though relieved by the vibrancy of David's faith, was still seeing the situation through a different lens. He thought the answer must lie in fighting Goliath on man's terms. So he offered David his armor, helmet, coat of mail, and sword. David "tried in vain to go," but he could not move easily, unaccustomed as he was to the armor. Saul's total reliance on these man-made methods of defense revealed where he put his trust—in human weapons and not in the living God. David, on the other hand, realized the foolishness of fighting with weapons that were merely cheap imitations of those of the Philistines. He must fight another way.

It was part of his tactical genius to choose the five smooth stones and his sling. It was the one weapon that, if used with incredible skill and perfect aim, could hit Goliath in the only place where he was vulnerable, the only place outside the protection of his armor—his forehead. But it would take nerves of steel on David's part and a bravery that would come not from youth, but from the highest possible motivation—deep trust and vibrant faith in the living God.

When Goliath approached David, he taunted as only a bully can. But David was undaunted. It was hard to imagine a more unequal, seemingly hopeless situation—this enormous, overly-armed Goliath lumbering toward this essentially unarmed boy. But what we see is the difference between the armor of man and the armor of God.

David gave his second speech in characteristic style—bold, full of faith, and unintimidated. "You come to me with the sword and the spear . . . but I come to you in the name of the living God, whom you have defied."

David clarified that the nature of the battle was theological at its core. Goliath had cursed David by his gods. David, in turn, made it clear that this fight would be not merely between two men, but between the true God of Israel and the false gods of the Philistines. "Yahweh will deliver you into my hand . . . that all the earth may know that Israel has a God who saves." According to David, the purpose of the battle was not only to defeat a Philistine, but to glorify God before the eyes of the world.

But even with David defending the true God, to an outsider it certainly looked like an unequal contest. Looks are deceiving, however, because the deck really was stacked in favor of the one "after God's own heart." David defeated Goliath before the Philistine ever made his first move. The only conclusion one can draw is that there was an extraordinary power operating beyond David's own power—namely, the faithful, living God.

What truths are we to learn from this story? We all want to keep our equilibrium when fear begins to drain and defeat us. How did David find such courage and hope in spite of the overwhelming odds against him? Is such fearlessness only for the privileged few? Or can we emulate his robust faith in fearful situations?

TWO FACES OF FEAR

Smart Fear

First, we must remember that not all fear is bad. In *The Republic* Plato said that courage is motivated by being fearful of the right thing. In *The Nicomachean Ethics* Aristotle said that to know something is destructive and harmful *should* produce fear. Courage, he said, is having the right amount of fear directed at the right object for the right reason.

The Bible says that the beginning of wisdom is the fear of the Lord. The commandment in Scripture to fear God—in other words, to live in awe, reverence, and deep respect before God—is not a sweet thought to have our grandmothers embroider for the kitchen wall. To fear God means that we take seriously the consequences of not obeying him.

Ironically, the one thing that will most stabilize and calm us when we are afraid is *fearing the right thing*—the Lord's opinion, the Lord's honor, and the Lord's judgment. All other fears must fall in line after that.

Dangerous Fear

Second, we must avoid giving in to the wrong kind of fear. Saul's main problem wasn't that he was afraid, but that he feared man rather than God. Jesus continually told his disciples to resist the wrong kind of fear. Indeed, one of his constant refrains was "Fear not." More than one writer has suggested that the message of the angels to terrified humans was nearly always: "There, there."

Fear is something we all struggle with at one time or another. Whether we are rich or poor, young or old, powerful or unprotected, a king or a hunted fugitive, we all wrestle with fearful impulses. Especially in a violent society like ours, no one is exempt, not even our children. I recently asked an elementary schoolboy how he liked his new school. I naively expected him to say what most boys his age said when I was growing up: "I like recess and P.E." But his immediate response was: "I like it better than my other school. I feel safer here." I thought I had misunderstood him, but he continued. "There were gangs in my last school. And riding the bus was scary." I left shaking my head in disbelief that we now live in a world where safety is a real uncertainty for a ten-year-old.

Besides the fear that is externally motivated by the violence and decay of our culture, there are inner fears that eat away at us also. We struggle with the fear of failure, the fear that maybe we don't have what it takes to be effective and successful personally and professionally. There may be a lingering deeper fear: does God *really* care about me? If push came to shove, would God choose someone else more worthy to love over me? These fears are common, but they need to be acknowledged and worked through. Because if they are not acknowledged, they will drive us in unhealthy ways.

I have a friend who is extraordinarily sensitive to the needs of others. God uses her in powerful ways to bring healing and understanding to many. One day I noticed she was uncharacteristically depressed. I probed gently to see what was wrong. She said, "I have been trying to help a friend in trouble and I can't seem to reach her. I know I am not God, and the Lord is perfectly capable of bringing someone else along who could help her. But I realized this morning what it was that was depressing me. It was fear. I had a teacher in high school who said, 'You will never amount to anything.' What was haunting me was that perhaps my inability to help my friend was just confirming the truth of what that teacher had said all along."

I couldn't imagine how she could believe for one second the

destructive lie that former teacher had spoken to her. Yet, upon reflection, I realized it is what we all do. Most of us are plagued with fears and doubts that outsiders would not believe even if we told them. But she added: "Once I realized what the culprit was, I acknowledged my fear to God. I asked forgiveness for believing the lie of that old judgment rather than the truth of who I am in Christ. It was then that I began to experience release from the fear."

RISK BEING REAL

What struck me as she spoke was the necessity of owning our fear, confessing it to God, and then choosing to believe the truth instead of the lie. If only Saul had done that. If only he had admitted not only his immediate fear—the real possibility that Israel would lose a strategic battle to the Philistines—but also the deeper fears that no doubt plagued him: *Do my men think I am a failure? Do I have what it takes to do my job well? What if I fail?*

Saul should have told God how he was feeling. Think about it. When you have risked sharing deep fears with a trusted friend and it has been received lovingly, what was the result? Didn't it deepen the intimacy between you? But Saul would not risk being real with God. God would not have been mad at him for being afraid, for he knew Saul was up against humanly impossible odds. But Saul was always too formal, too polite, too careful with God to ever voice his fears. And without that kind of honesty before his Creator, he ended up with no reality of faith. Saul's unspoken fears paralyzed him.

We may read this story and think, *That Saul, what a wimp! He should have had faith!* Saul clearly needed to have faith. But Saul's situation was truly terrifying. So how does one go about obtaining the faith that conquers fear? Ironically, it is by *refusing to pretend*. It is by admitting to God that we are terrified and we aren't sure we have the faith necessary for the battle. But we never see that kind of reality in Saul's relationship to the Lord.

Many years ago when I worked for InterVarsity Christian Fellowship, I was invited to do an evangelistic outreach on a campus in Indiana. I was to give an evangelistic address on Friday evening, to which the Christian students were to bring their spiritually seeking, skeptic friends. Several of my coworkers and I came early to train the InterVarsity students in how to share their faith. We, the staff, were excited and thrilled with the potential of what God might do. However, it did not take long before I realized that the mission was likely to be a complete flop. Because as I looked at the faces of those Christian students, it was clear they were terrified.

When I began the training session in preparation for the Friday night event, the students listened with polite reservation. But what changed the tide was a delightfully honest coed who suddenly blurted out, "Look, the bottom line is this: I don't want my friends to think I'm weird. I know they respect me now. But if I invite them to come and this ends up being really dorky and they decide I'm a loser, they might reject me. And besides . . . I don't know quite how to say this, but . . . *What if you're a lousy speaker?!*" And with that she burst into tears. Suddenly all the rest of the students poured out their genuine fears.

After listening to them I said, "You know, five minutes ago I was sure this was going to be a flop. But after seeing the risk you just took by being so honest, I think it's going to be just the opposite. Thank you with all my heart for not being polite and religious with me. God isn't mad at you for being scared. He understands. But he can't help you unless you are willing to be honest with him. God cares not only that your friends will hear the Gospel on Friday, but he wants your own faith to be strengthened as well. There are two things that cause faith to grow: acknowledging your fears and doubts, and then being willing to take a risk in spite of them. If you take the risk to invite someone, I know God will honor your faith. The truth is, even if I totally bomb on Friday, God won't let you down. He honors faith. So take a risk for God and invite a friend." What started out as a mission "to them" began to be perceived as a faith-growing venture "for us."

Those students took the risk and brought their friends, not only to the first night but every subsequent night. Students became Christians, Bible studies got started, and Christian students were strengthened in their confidence in God. They saw God come through in ways they could not have imagined. Very few campus missions stand out in my memory with greater joy than that one. But the power of it lay in students facing their fear, confessing it, and then taking the risk of obedience.

Aristotle wrote that courage is not the absence of fear, but the ability to operate in the face of fear. (*The Nicomachean Ethics,* Book IV) If only Saul had trusted God with his fear and taken a risk like those students did. But he did not.

Saul knew better. He had been taught by the prophet Samuel that Israel's power did not lie in its military strength but in the power of Yahweh. Yet when the crisis with Goliath arose, Saul listened not to the voice of God, but to the taunts and boasts of Goliath, whose campaign was typical of an oppressor: psychological warfare through intimidation.

We don't fault the king for seeing how grave his situation was, or even for feeling fearful. Saul was a seasoned warrior. He knew that he was up against humanly impossible odds. But the human impossibility of his situation should have driven him to his knees before God. However, there is no record of Saul praying in this crisis. Instead, he did what most of us do when we forget God is in charge—he interpreted reality only by what he could see. And the fear that resulted paralyzed him and his army. It was a colossal failure of faith on his part.

DON'T FEAR APPEARANCES

If there is an all-powerful, loving God who is accomplishing his purposes behind the scenes, then we must never look at our present circumstances and conclude that what we see is all there is to reality. No matter what life looks like presently, no matter how much it appears that evil is winning, humans don't have the last word. God has the last word, and it is a word of hope, peace, and victory to those who love him and who are walking in his will. But God's purposes take time to work out. So what we need while we wait for God's answer is patience and courage that comes from robust faith, and an absolute, flat-out refusal to believe that what we see is what we get.

Without a strong confidence in God, Saul couldn't perceive reality through the eyes of faith. He may have believed intellectually, but his faith wasn't operative at the practical level where he needed it the most. All Saul did was despair over what he could see—the relative size of David and Goliath, and the discrepancies between their weapons, age, and experience. But it wasn't only a matter of trusting in appearances; it was *believing the lie* that got Saul into even more serious trouble.

DON'T FEAR SATAN'S LIES

Saul teaches us our first lesson about fear: that if we fail to believe the truth—in this case, that we can overcome the "giants" in our lives through God's strength—then we will believe the lie, that people and circumstances ultimately dictate the outcome rather than God's grace. The fact is, *we will believe in something,* and it will either be true or false. Fear is conquered when we believe the truth and trust in God. So when we are embattled and feel our spiritual courage melting, we need to ask ourselves if we are embracing a lie that is empowering evil and blocking our faith.

Goliath teaches us something valuable too: that the style of evil is often noisy and boisterous. Goliath's arrogance and self-confidence— the pride that goes before the fall—prove that there is an illusory nature to evil. It attempts to win by bluff, by puffing itself up to horrendous size through intimidation. Its style is frightening, but Saul shows us that the real danger lies not in the threat itself, but in giving the evil threat "life" by believing it. Evil can be prolonged, fed, and empowered when we trust our terrified impulses rather than turning to God in faith.

Remember God's Deliverance

The remedy to fear will be discussed in chapter 2. However when waves of anxiety threaten to overwhelm us we need to remember how God has rescued us previously in fearful times. Remembering his deliverance will strengthen our faith and give us fresh courage as we face present difficulties. Once I was flying home for Christmas break during my sophomore year in college. I had been a Christian for nearly two years, but spiritual doubts had begun to fester in my mind. I tried to pray, but I was not certain that God was as personal as I had assumed or even that he was there. I confided in a friend before I boarded the airplane that I was in spiritual crisis. But I did not know what to do.

I had a five-hour layover in St. Louis, so I decided to go to a nearby mall for some last-minute Christmas shopping. The airport was jammed with people, and once I got outside I asked a man if he knew where the taxi-cab waiting area was. He said, "Oh, I'm a cab driver. Let me take you." "Great," I responded, thinking how lucky I was as I followed him to his car. As we approached the vehicle, I saw that there was no marker identifying it as a taxi. "My cab is in the garage, and I really do need to make some money," he said. It was late, and I was young and naive, and of course tired from just having finished final exams. But the minute I stepped into his car, I knew he wasn't a cab driver, and I knew that I was in serious trouble.

He sped away quickly, and I kept reiterating how glad I was that the mall was so close. But the mall never appeared, and soon he was driving farther and farther away from traffic. I remember the sickening feeling in the pit of my stomach as I looked out the back window of the car, watching all the traffic lights fading away. Suddenly we were on a lonely country road, with no other cars and no one to cry out to for any help. For the first time in months I prayed, a silent desperate prayer for God's help. The thought that came to me was, "Tell him of my love."

I began to talk a mile a minute. I told him about me, how I had become a Christian, and even what the Lord had done in my life. I shared that I was going home for Christmas and couldn't wait to see my parents and brother and sister. I asked him to tell me about himself and his family, though he did not answer. Never mind! I talked enough for both of us. Then there was a chilling moment. He pulled the car to the side of the road and stared at me through the rearview mirror. There was nothing more I could say, and so I waited in silent prayer. After what felt like an eternity, he turned the car around and without ever saying a word, drove me to the shopping mall and dropped me off. When we arrived I tried to pay him, but he said, "I think you know that is ridiculous." I thanked him for returning me, and then I asked him to consider the Lord, but I was so frightened that I couldn't say much else.

I could not stop shaking once I knew I was safe. I called a real taxi service and returned to the airport immediately. I told the driver what had happened, and of course he lectured me severely for being so foolish as to get into an unmarked car. Then he said, "Now, I need to tell you something. Last week at this airport, a pleasant-looking man told a young woman that his taxi was in the shop, and that he needed the money badly. And she fell for it. He then took her to a country road and raped and stabbed her repeatedly. She's in critical condition at the hospital and the police haven't been able to find him. Let me tell you, girly, Somebody up there likes you."

I thought I was shaky after the incident, but upon hearing that story I sat down on a bench outside of the airport, just to calm my nerves. And then I prayed a prayer that today makes me incredulous. I said, "God, I never thought that after my conversion I would be troubled again by such deep doubts. But that's where I am. I want with all my heart to believe that it was you who just spared my life. I have no right to ask this, but would you please confirm that it was you? *Please, Lord, I need to know that you are there."*

I walked inside and went to the coffee shop and sat down at the counter. A very distinguished-looking, gray-haired man was sitting next to me. He had deep, kind eyes. He asked me if I was a college student, and we made some small talk. Then he began to talk very gently about the real meaning of Christmas. I said, "Yes, I believe in God, too. But I think Christianity is basically just the ethic of loving one another. Don't you?"

I waited for his answer, but in my soul I cried out, *Oh please, tell me it's more, tell me it's much more. Tell me the truth.* And then he said, "Well, love is certainly central, but apart from Jesus dying and being raised from the dead, and apart from an intimate relationship with him, we can't hope to be transformed by the love you are talking about."

Those words felt like warm oil being poured over me. I then told him what had just happened. He walked me to my plane, and his final words to me were, "Becky, God just saved your life. That's quite a Christmas present I'd say. The Lord bless you, Becky."

I boarded that plane and knew beyond any question that God had spoken. He was real and he was there. God had delivered me from evil and kept me from enormous danger, but even more powerfully, he confirmed it through one of his servants. And though it may seem small to someone else, no one had ever before said to me, "The Lord bless you, Becky." It wasn't just that God was personal and powerful, but he loved me like a father. I cried all the way home.

That man's name was Charles Hatfield, a mathematics professor at the University of Missouri. He is now in heaven, and although I was able to thank him once many years later, I doubt it was until he saw the Lord that he realized the enormity of the impact that he and that one cup of coffee had on my life.

There have been other fearful times in my life since then. And the temptation in each new trial was to underestimate God and overestimate evil. We assume that because we don't always see what God is doing that he is doing nothing. And because we see everything that evil is doing, we feel our fate is left dangling. We cannot afford to be naive. Our problem must be faced realistically and squarely. But when we are in a fearful situation, there is nothing that builds our confidence in God more than remembering his promises: "Do not be fainthearted or afraid; do not be terrified or give way to panic. . . . For the Lord your God is the one who goes with you to fight for you against your enemies to give you victory." (Deut. 20:3b-4)

QUESTIONS AND REFLECTIONS

1. What are the things you fear that are of Goliath-sized proportion in your life?
2. Is there a noticeable pattern to these things you fear?
3. Can you identify a lie you have believed that might be empowering your fear?

4. Is your fear tied to something you are trying to control, something you need to let go of? Is it something that you could never control anyway?

5. Remember God's character. Find seven verses (one for each day of the week) about God's character, write them out on index cards, and consider your problem in light of the verses you've chosen. If you need help locating appropriate passages, consult a Bible concordance and reference verses under the character trait of God that you feel you most need to familiarize yourself with right now.

Chapter Two

Faith:
The Remedy for Fear

How would you answer the question, "What is the remedy to fear?" It is easy to think that the answer to fear lies in developing courage. But courage is a funny thing—we can't increase it by trying. That's because courage is a by-product of something else.

David's courage, for example, wasn't the result of having a positive mental attitude. We don't see David running around to the soldiers saying, "Hey, guys, *where's your enthusiasm?* Let's whip up a little of the ol' positive attitude! Just think warm thoughts and I *know* we can win!" David's confidence did not rest in his powerful or persuasive personality, or even in his ability to be courageous. David's courage was the direct result of his *faith in God.* It was David's bedrock confidence in God that helped him triumph in a very difficult situation.

So if faith produces courage that helps us conquer fear, then the question is, how do we strengthen our faith?

BUILDING FAITH

Remember What Is True

David showed us that when the odds truly are against us and we feel overwhelmed, the single most important thing we can ever do is to remember what is most real—the character, power and rule of God.

It's a question of "first things first," getting our vision of God clarified before anything else. Our immediate problem must be understood in the larger picture of who God is and what his purposes are. In other words, *faith conquers fear.*

It is astonishing to watch even believers walk through crisis and pain, muscling their way through and trying to be brave. But God never intended for us to go through difficult times alone. He has given us resources that enable us to overcome. We know this is true in the physical realm. Shortly after we begin exercising, we are surprised at how much better we feel, and at our renewed capacity to cope with stress. This is equally true in the spiritual realm. God has given us the provisions with which to strengthen our faith, but they can't help us if we don't use them.

Remember God's Character

Faith that conquers fear comes by remembering our Creator. When Jesus' disciples were frightened by the murderous threats of the ruling leaders of the Sanhedrin, what was the first thing they did? They "remembered"—even before they acted. They prayed, and their prayer began not by reminding God of their problem, but by reminding *themselves* of the nature and character of God. In the midst of a terrifying situation they cried out: "Sovereign Lord." In other words, "Oh Lord, the One who is in charge of all creation and who overrules all of history . . . we trust you in our present problem!" As they prayed, they recited God's characteristics: *"You made"* (he is the God of creation), *"You spoke"* (he is the God of revelation), and *"You anointed"* (he is the God of history). This God so overrules human history that when people conspired to have Jesus crucified, it looked for a moment like evil had won the day. But "they did what your power and will had decided beforehand should happen." Then, after this lengthy preamble, the disciples finally mentioned the problem: "Consider their threats."

It is a faithful prayer, but it is also a wise prayer model to follow when we are afraid. Our focus should be on God before our problems. We must remember who God is and how his faithfulness has been evident throughout the course of our lives.

We must also keep in mind that all of life is under the reign and rule of a sovereign Lord. Nothing is more important to understand in a crisis of fear than knowing this. Sanhedrins may sputter and threaten, giants may curse and intimidate, people may act as if they are morally autonomous and subject to none, but no one and nothing is capable of overturning the will of God. "There may be times when people do not see clearly. Blinded by sin and perhaps even by pathology, they thumb their noses at all that is sacred to life, like Goliath did, and, eventually, Saul. But it does not matter how much bluster or skilled slyness our enemies possess, the only reality that matters is God's.

THE VALUE OF SCRIPTURE

Another vital resource that calms our fears and builds our faith is the Bible. Yet the amount of biblical illiteracy in the church is astonishing. In a recent Gallup survey given to churchgoers to test their knowledge of Scripture, 50 percent could not name the first book of the Bible. Two out of three did not know the names of the four Gospels. Another research group that conducted a similar survey asked, "Who preached the Sermon on the Mount?" One churchgoer responded, "Someone on a horse?"

Perhaps our resistance to Bible reading comes from having seen Scripture used superficially, like a simple Band-Aid for every complex problem of life. I have a friend whose mother was converted in her later years. Her mother was a woman of enormous strength and a delightful force to be reckoned with. When she came to faith in Christ, she was, as one would expect, unabashedly enthusiastic. Once she finally read the Bible for herself, she was determined that everyone she came in contact with would also read it. So she took a pair of scissors, cut up every verse in the Bible, and put the verses in a huge box. Whenever she gave a gift, she'd blindly pull out a verse and throw it into the gift box. Then, she'd insist that the person opening the gift read the verse aloud. Sometimes a verse was appropriate, but more often than not, these gift-openings were an occasion no one wanted to miss. Like the time one recipient politely tried to cover her horrified expression by saying, "Oh, thank you so very much. But, ah, I was just wondering . . . what exactly does it mean, 'Each will feed on the flesh of his own offspring'"? (Isa. 9:20b) Or when someone read, "And the King rose and Bernice and those sitting with them." (Acts 26:30) He asked, "Excuse me, but am I missing some deeper religious meaning here?" Or the time an avowed agnostic read, with eyes as wide as saucers, that "the people expected him to swell up or suddenly fall dead, but after waiting a long time and seeing nothing unusual happen to him, they changed their minds and said he was a god." (Acts 28:6) But no matter the verse, my friend's mother would always say in her irrepressible style, "Hey! Don't look at me—I didn't write it! Anyway, it's *the Bible!* So it's gotta be good for you."

Of course we know that anyone can prove almost anything by taking verses out of context. That is why it is so important to read a single verse in the context of the larger passage, and then the passage in light of the whole Bible. But when we think of the immense wisdom, power, and encouragement of God's revelatory principles for living—principles that we discover by Scripture reading—the question is, Why don't we read the Bible to build our faith?

FAITH COMES BY BELIEVING GOD'S WORD

How can knowing the Bible and trusting that it is true increase faith and strengthen our courage when we are afraid? How has trusting God's Word helped other believers in fearful times? The apostle Paul is a good example. He longed to go to Rome to preach the Gospel. But before he could get there he was imprisoned in Jerusalem. He was falsely accused and slandered by his own Jewish leaders, which put him up against Jerusalem *and* Rome, the two strongest power blocs in the ancient world. The likelihood that a solitary dissident like Paul could overcome their combined might was next to nil.

Think of it. Is the problem that's causing you fear right now as serious as having both the church authorities and the state authorities standing ready to kill you? The odds couldn't have been more terrifyingly against Paul. He had experienced two very violent days from his attackers, and no doubt he was feeling deeply anxious over his situation. It almost certainly looked as if Paul would be executed shortly. Yet this never seemed to enter Paul's mind as a possibility. Why?

Because during Paul's prison stay, Jesus appeared, stood near Paul in his prison cell, and spoke. "Take courage! As you have testified about me in Jerusalem, so you must also testify in Rome."

It would be hard to exaggerate the kind of rock-steady courage Jesus' words gave Paul. Still, it is interesting to note what Jesus *didn't* say. The Lord did not elaborate by saying, "Paul, you are going to Rome, but before you get there, be prepared! You will have to spend more time in the slammer, you will be in a near-fatal storm at sea, you will have to defend yourself in trials, men will plot to kill you, and you'll get bitten by a snake." No, the Lord only told him, "You will go to Rome."

Even if what we have of Jesus' words to Paul is merely a summary, the point is still the same. Jesus wanted Paul to know that when he spoke, Paul could count on it being true. Yet we almost find ourselves wishing that Jesus had dramatically emphasized what he said to Paul. "Listen, Paul, you're going to Rome, and I really, *really* mean it." We tend to forget that when you are God, you don't have to say a whole lot. The character of God is trustworthy, which means his words are reliable. Paul knew that, and he trusted what Jesus said to him as if his life depended upon it, which, of course, it did. Paul overcame his fear because he believed, as Isaiah says, that "the grass withers, the flower fades, but the word of the Lord endures forever."

Why didn't Jesus tell Paul more? Because God was building Paul's faith and character in the midst of terrifying circumstances, just as he is building ours. One of the reasons God does not give us a detailed game plan ahead of time is because he is in the process of building people who will live with him for eternity. And eternity must be inhabited by people who have chosen to trust and love God based on his words; who have learned through their fearful experiences on earth that he is absolutely trustworthy.

But we may say, "I wouldn't fear either if Jesus would come and speak to *me* the way he spoke to Paul." God may not choose to visit us with an audible voice, but here is the point: He does not have to.

Already God has spoken to us through his Word. And his Word will bring comfort and calm in the terror of the night, more than a thousand well-intended human words ever could. The question is, how can God reveal himself to us if we will not bother to read what he says?

FAITH COMES BY LIVING GOD'S WORD

As we learn to rely upon the truth of the Bible, it becomes a moral compass in a confusing, unstable, and often scary world. Scripture not only guides us into *orthodoxy* (right thinking), but also into *orthopraxis* (right living). Our obedience to God's Word will keep us steady in the worst of times.

The old adage is true that we cannot break the law; we only break ourselves when we violate the moral principles or laws that govern God's universe. We have every reason to fear if we have knowingly violated God's commandments with unrepentant hearts. We may try to bolster our courage by reciting faith verses, but if we are deliberately living outside of divine moral laws, we can be sure that eventually we will crash.

If we are walking obediently, on the other hand, confessing our sins regularly and living in the light as best we know how, God's Word will give us the courage we need when times are difficult. The resolution to our situation may take time, and the road may be treacherous, but our courage comes from knowing that the road map we have submitted to is completely trustworthy. Courage that conquers fear comes when we do as the old hymn tells us: "Trust and obey, for there's no other way."

FAITH COMES FROM USING GOD'S WORD

One of the things that makes us fearful is tangible evil. However, we need to always keep in mind that God's Word is a powerful weapon to defeat evil. When we are afraid we must fight back in faith, and we must stand on God's promises *regardless* of what we are feeling. That is how the devil is resisted—when we stand on what God says and *not* on what we can see or feel. In fearful times we must shout aloud God's promises and live their truth for all our worth.

Determine that the next time you are assailed with fear and anxieties you will verbalize God's promises. "Be strong, do not fear; your God will come." "My grace is sufficient for you." "All things work together for good to them that love God." "The joy of the Lord is my strength." "The peace of God, which transcends all understanding, will guard your hearts and minds in Christ Jesus." God's Word is a powerful weapon that defeats fear and gives courage. If only Saul had chosen to respond in faith. If only he had declared, "Be strong and courageous. Do not be terrified; do not be discouraged, for the Lord your God will be with you wherever you go." (Josh. 1:9)

THE WEAPONS OF FAITH

Instead, it is David who demonstrates for us that faith isn't merely an esoteric intellectual exercise. David's faith enabled him to understand the deeper nature of the battle with Goliath as well as the kind of practical weapons he needed to do battle in an effective way.

Choosing the Right Weapons; Recognizing the Real Battle

David teaches us a vital lesson about the weapons we must use for life's battles. We are not to fight the Lord's battles with the Devil's tools. The primary objective of evil is engagement on its own terms. If we respond by taking the bait, we only end up in the cesspool along with our enemies. We must remain above the fray and refuse to resort to their tactics, just as David did.

To an outsider, the battle looked like the mere defeat of a bully. But David made it clear that the purpose of this victory was not only to bring the defeat of Goliath, but ultimately to bring glory to God in the eyes of the world. The conflict between David and Goliath demonstrated how human battles have deeper purposes. We must remember, therefore, that in the midst of battle the Lord delivers not with the conventions of human warfare but with his own weapons and in his own ways.

What were the divine weapons that David used with Goliath? David, it seems, was a precursor to Ephesians chapter 6. There, the apostle Paul instructs us to put on the spiritual armor of God for life's battles.

In David's battle, the first stone to be slung was not a rock, but rather, words of truth. One word of truth, spoken in the power of the Holy Spirit, flies like a rock to puncture evil's swelled balloon of lies.

Goliath had a sword, a spear, and a javelin—the conventional sort of arms—while David had none of these things. But he had the powerful name of Yahweh, whom Goliath had defied. David stated the truth as sharply as possible: he would win this battle because "the Lord will deliver you into my hand." David was armed with God's truth, and this enabled him to be rightly attuned to reality and to see the deception of Goliath's boasts.

David's breastplate, while not visible, was one of righteousness. He was not defending his own righteousness, but the righteousness of God. David was incensed, not because he had been demeaned and insulted, but because God had been mocked.

David had no physical shield, but nevertheless he stepped out in a shield of faith when no one else dared to do so. He knew his only source of help was God. Faith enabled David to look straight to God for the victory.

David did not wear a helmet of metal but one of salvation; he believed the purpose of the battle was "that all of this assembly may know there is a true God in Israel."

David revealed that victory comes when we use weapons designed for the nature of the battle in which we are engaged. Seemingly so vulnerable and unprepared for fighting this well-equipped giant, David was, as it turned out, much more fully armed for the battle than Goliath. "The weapons we fight with are not the weapons of the world. On the contrary, they have divine power to demolish strongholds." (2 Cor. 10:4) "For our struggle is not against flesh and blood, but against the rulers, against the authorities, against the powers of this dark world and against the spiritual forces of evil in the heavenly realms." (Eph. 6:12) The most powerful weapons of life are the invisible weapons of the Spirit.

The Bible and spiritual armor, then, are two of the resources God has given us to build a faith that leads to courage and enables us to conquer fear. But are the only weapons available to us in times of fear ones of a spiritual nature?

Of course not! David was a profoundly spiritual man, yet we don't find that he walked into battle, smiled beatifically, and said, "My battle motto is 'just let go and let God.' I'm going to claim in faith that God will give Goliath a coronary." David took practical steps as he approached this crisis situation.

Be Resourceful and Use Your Best Option

Faith is not plastering on a superficial smile while we grimly rearrange the deck chairs on the *Titanic*. To have faith means we take responsibility for what we can while using the best option available to us, and then leave the rest to God.

David's attitude was anything but that of a victim. Instead of throwing his hands up in despair, he evaluated his available resources and the circumstances, chose his weapon wisely, and then expected God to make up the difference. We usually complain that *our* resources are too inadequate to make a difference. But that is the very point! God delights in demonstrating his power through our limitations and inadequacies.

When Jesus gathered his team of disciples, he may have longed for at least one theologian in the bunch. But the Lord chose from the men available, and look at what was accomplished! Whatever the nature of the "giants" that we battle, we must begin with the resources we have and use the weapons available to us. Always remember that situations of comparative inadequacy are God's specialty!

TAKE RESPONSIBILITY AND ACT!

There is a time to talk, pray, strategize, project—and even to budget. But eventually we have to *do* something. The tendency of fear is to do everything *but* act. David wasn't impulsive. He explored the problem and he listened to all the advice. But finally, he took action.

The only way ultimately to conquer our fears is to follow David's example: ask God for help, and then boldly confront the "giants" in our lives. Spirit-led action defeats the power that our fears have over us. And this fortifies us in the truth.

BE PREPARED, BUT LEAVE THE RESULTS TO GOD

The courage David demonstrated against Goliath revealed not only the power of God, but the other side of the coin—that "practice makes perfect." Where did David's enormous courage come from? Was his an "on the spot" response?

One might be able to muster courage once or twice in an impromptu way. But the depth of courage and faith that *David* demonstrated shows that he certainly had some prior training in these areas. Where did David get his "practice sessions" in courage?

When Saul insisted that David was too young to fight a bully like Goliath, David explained that as a lad tending sheep he had had to protect his flock and himself from lions and bears. "The Lord who delivered me from the paw of the lion and the paw of the bear will deliver me from the hand of this Philistine."

Now in David's day, being a shepherd was probably the ancient equivalent to being a parking lot attendant. His job held absolutely no status. It was looked upon as a menial and even a trivial way to spend one's time. But as we watch him face Goliath, we marvel at his skill in handling a bully terrifying God's sheep. It is clear that David's courage was developed during his shepherd years.

All of this tells us something very important about life. When we consider people who have their moment in the sun—athletes, per-formers, authors, academics, scientists, or even heroes like David—we often assume they were born with such extraordinary skill that whatever they accomplished came naturally. But that is almost never the case. Naturally gifted though they are, their moment in the public eye usually required years of obscurity and training. Their public life was preceded by an unglamorous private life. What this tells us is that life is not a cram-course in character. The skills needed for it are built, not in a weekend, but in years and years of weekends—and weekdays!

Therefore, we must see those boring, routine aspects of our hidden life as being of equal, if not greater, importance than our public life. Little could David have imagined as he fought wild animals alone in the wilderness that it was actually boot camp for another bully yet to come. Only on the occasion of his meeting Goliath, he wouldn't be alone; he'd feel as if the whole world watched. Little did he dream that people would still be watching 3,000 years later.

How do we develop faith that produces courage, faith that overcomes our fears? Certainly not by waiting idly for our great moment in the sun, where we dash in before thousands to prove our mettle. No, our mettle will be formed in the ordinary moments of life. Character comes from doing the mundane tasks and routine duties that lie before us, and doing them to the best of our ability for the glory of God. God prepared David for great things, but did not expect him to respond with profound faith and courage all at once. Instead, God gave David one experience after another to build his faith and character. He will do the same for us.

DEEP ROOTS MAKE ALL THE DIFFERENCE

What will we be like as we grow in faith and respond with courage, rather than caving in to fear? When I think of courage rooted in faith, I think of the strongest trees in existence, the Sequoias that grow close to the ocean. They are strong because they have had to endure so many gale winds over the years. Consequently, their roots have grown very deep, and their branches are extremely sturdy.

In the first Psalm we are told that the righteous person is like "a tree planted by streams of water, which yields its fruit in season and whose leaf does not wither. Whatever he does prospers." The Christian who is rooted in God can withstand the buffeting of the wind and will flourish regardless of the storms. He will offer fruit and shade and blessing to everyone he comes in contact with. He is like the house Jesus spoke of—the rains came and beat upon the house, but it withstood the test because it was built on solid rock.

Conversely, the psalmist tells us that those who do *not* walk in God's ways are like chaff, the translucent cover over the kernel of grain. Chaff is so light it is weightless, and is carried away by the small-

est wind. The image here is powerful. Will we settle for being weightless chaff, or will our faith and courage be the strong, firm substance
of a Sequoia?

Milos Kundera, the Czechoslovakian novelist, wrote a story where
he assumes that Nietzsche was right when he argued that it was senseless to claim a moral meaning in a world without God. Kundera's conclusion was that because God does not exist, humanity has no
meaning. And truly, without God, we are doomed to a state of *The
Unbearable Lightness of Being,* which is what he titled the novel.

The psalmist agrees wholeheartedly that weightlessness defines
exactly a life separated from God. Fear reduces us to chaff: "Peter,
Satan has demanded to have you that he may sift you like
wheat."(Luke 22:31) But God intends to use fearful circumstances to
make us into trees: "You meant it for evil, but God meant it for
good."(Gen. 50:20)

In the south of France there is a little village called Le Chambon.
There was a pacifist Protestant pastor in Le Chambon named Andre
Trocme. During the Nazi occupation, Trocme faithfully preached the
Gospel and encouraged the people of his village to protect the Jews.
Most of these villagers had small farms, and they led very simple lives.
Yet they hid Jews in their homes, gave them identity cards (often with
different names), incorporated the Jewish children into their schools,
gave the adults jobs, and shared their food. It was not uncommon for
these villagers to answer a knock at their doors only to hear their pastor saying, "Three Old Testaments have arrived" (which was the code
name for Jews). No one was turned away. As a result, five thousand
villagers saved around five thousand Jewish lives.

And it was all done in full view of the Vichy government with the
knowledge that if they were caught they would be killed or sent to concentration camps.

Thirty years later a young Jewish film director, Pierre Sauvage,
whose family (himself included) had been hidden by a Christian Le
Chambonaise family, decided to return to the village to find out
what had motivated these people to help the Jews. Why did they act
so bravely when most of the Christian world remained tragically

silent during the Holocaust? The filmmaker went back to interview the men and women who helped, most of them by then in their seventies and eighties.

His interviews revealed people of enormous character, whose inner stillness and serenity shone through. They were incredibly gentle and gracious, yet tough-minded about what was important. There was no intellectualizing, no excusing, no debating about right and wrong. When the test came, they acted. Their faith wasn't sentimental; it was solid and not found wanting. And they had humor, as evidenced by one farmer who during that time had named his pig "Adolf."

They did not have facile answers for why they helped the Jews. In fact, they found it odd that anyone would think of them as heroes. "I helped because they needed to be helped. In the Bible it is written to feed the hungry. To visit the sick. That is a normal thing to do," responded Madame Barraud. A Madame Brottes was asked why she wasn't more fearful for her life. "You can't talk about faith if you do not act . . . if you give nothing to your brother, you're a wretched soul. And the neighbor you must love as yourself is in the street. We mustn't act like the priest who saw the man who had fallen among thieves and who passed by on the other side. And the Jew, truly, had fallen among thieves."

No community in France was more defiantly opposed to the Vichy government than the village of Le Chambon. Their courage came, in part, from their Huguenot heritage, a heritage familiar with persecution. When the government sent a Vichy Minister on an official visit, the villagers listened to his speech. But when the Vichy official, standing next to the Marshal, finished with the usual cry of "Long live Marshal Petain!" there was dead silence before someone shouted back, "Long live Jesus Christ!" Then the teenagers of the village handed the Minister a letter telling him the villagers refused to make a distinction between Jews and non-Jews, and they made it clear they would seek to hide any Jews the government tried to deport. Then they invited the officials to attend their church service. Madame Brottes remembers that day well: "There was a very good moment. The church was full . . . and we sang a hymn in honor of the persecuted.

We sang it! And if they had lined us up against a wall, we were ready to face the machine guns."

The Le Chambon villagers and their pastor are prime examples of the courage that comes from faith in Jesus Christ. Fear causes us to focus on ourselves and our own protection. Faith—and the action that results—forces us to focus on others. The people of Le Chambon acted bravely because their lives were unself-consciously and quietly devoted to God. Their faith was their antidote to fear.

What will we be like as we grow in faith, learning to choose courage and resist fear? Sauvage told Bill Moyers that his rather tough-minded, no-nonsense agnostic cousin visited Le Chambon during the time he conducted the interviews. At one point he introduced this cousin to Madame Brottes. After a delightful conversation, the eighty-one-year-old Brottes hugged her. Sauvage was flabbergasted to see his cousin suddenly break into tears. "You must have been very moved," Sauvage said to her. She replied, "Oh, Pierre, when she hugged me it was like hugging a tree."

God wants to form us into trees that will not wither in the storms of life. He will not keep us from experiencing these fierce times, but he *will* protect us from their power to destroy us. In fact, it is because of the storms that our roots will grow deep into the soil of Christ and give sustenance and fruit for others, in season and out of season.

Saul was scared senseless by Goliath, never realizing that even giants, with all their enormous armor, are still under the authority and control of the living God. No power in heaven or on earth can prevail against God. Human appearances count for nothing in light of the unseen power of the Almighty.

Poor Saul. If only he had had the eyes to see that Goliath, for all his size and noise and human strength and bravado, was really only chaff after all.

"At least there is hope for a tree: If it is cut down, it will sprout again, and its new shoots will not fail. Its roots may grow old in the ground and its stump die in the soil, yet at the scent of water it will bud and put forth shoots like a plant." (Job 14:7-9)

QUESTIONS AND REFLECTIONS

1. Remember how God helped you in anxious times before. Tell someone about it.

2. Pray these psalms when you feel afraid: 27, 37, 46, 91, and 112. Also, Deuteronomy 6:2, Exodus 20:20, and 1 John 4:18.

3. Verbalize the promises of God out loud, especially when you are assailed by a "fiery dart" of fear. Build your faith by speaking these promises out loud: Jeremiah 29:11-13; Isaiah 50:2, 59:1; Malachi 3:10; Mark 11:22; and Hebrews 11: 6.

4. Sing the hymn "A Mighty Fortress Is Our God" when you are afraid.

Chapter
Three

Envy:
A Sure Road
to Self-Destruction

H ave you ever secretly wished that someone envied you? Don't.
It is like harboring a death wish. Especially in our interpersonal
relationships.

At a conference where I was speaking, I met a woman who told
me she constantly compared herself to her older sister. This woman
was clearly gifted, bright, and attractive, but none of that mattered
because she didn't feel she was her sister's equal. She befriended people she wasn't really interested in while keeping a running tally on her
sister's social engagements. Her fear was that her sister might get a
slight social edge. It was clear her motive in life was not doing what
she truly enjoyed, but merely overtaking her sister. She had no peace
and no joy. She was miserable. Yet, though the problem was apparent,
she asked, "What do you think it is about my sister that makes me
respond in this way?"

Interestingly, her sister happened to attend the same conference
and told me her own pain. "All I want is to have a loving and close
relationship with my sister. But I feel my every move is being scruti-
nized. She is so critical and judgmental of me. The more I try to ignore
the put-downs and be kind, the nastier she gets. All I want is a relationship, but I feel like she's in a competitive race without realizing that
she's running alone—because I never entered it."

A conference setting wasn't the time to probe the obvious questions of whether one of their parents favored the older sister or whether as a child the younger was compared to the older. The roots of envy often begin in early life, especially when we are compared so often to others. And the basis of the comparisons are usually unfair because they concern areas over which we have no control. Who's more attractive, smarter, or more gifted? But envy's fruit was evident, for it produced misery and unhappiness for this woman and her family.

NEED AN EXAMPLE?

Literature, of course, is full of examples of the destructiveness of envy, whether it is Shakespeare's Iago who envied Othello's success and beautiful wife, Desdemona, or Snow White's envious stepmother. They testify to the utter destructiveness of wanting to possess the same "advantages" perceived in others. The Bible is also full of case studies on envy. Lucifer's revolt from heaven had its origin in envy as well as pride. Cain's murder of his brother, Abel, was rooted in envy. Herod's envy of a new king led to a massacre of innocent children. And the mother who falsely claimed to King Solomon that someone else's child was hers was envious of the actual mother of the baby. So deep and cruel was her envy that she preferred the child dead rather than allow someone else to enjoy what she lacked.

SAUL: THE PICTURE OF ENVY

However, no biblical example reveals the destructive pathos of envy as clearly as Saul's relentless pursuit of David. It may seem remarkable to the reader that this story, written before the birth of modern therapeutic insight, could be expressed with such psychological depth. Yet the biblical narrator offers such a bone-chilling description of Saul's slow progression from consumptive envy into paranoia and madness that it could provide therapists enough material to last a lifetime. We are allowed to see firsthand not only what a diseased perception of reality looks like, but we witness the terrifying consequences of his envy. Just watching what happens to Saul is high motivation to learn from his tragic failure.

Saul was Israel's first king. He was appointed through Samuel, the last of the great judges of Israel. Saul began as a brave, modest man, who had so much going for him, but he reached beyond the limits of his position as God's representative to the people of Israel. What made Saul especially vulnerable to envy was that he knew his days as king were numbered. The prophet Samuel told Saul that God deeply regretted making him king, because in two prior incidents Saul had disobeyed God's clear command.

SAUL'S FIRST FAILURE (1 SAMUEL 13)

The first time was an incident in which the Philistines were ready to attack the Israelites. Saul's men were very afraid, and Saul knew he must make a move soon if the whole army was not to desert. But he couldn't attack before Samuel the prophet came to offer the sacrifices that preceded battle—an act that traditionally demonstrated Israel's dependence on the Lord. Evidently there was an understanding that Samuel would come in seven days. Saul was on pins and needles as he waited for Samuel to arrive. Saul undoubtedly wanted to do the right thing. He waited for the seven days, but then his patience ran out. When the prophet didn't show, Saul took matters into his own hands and consecrated the burnt offering. With impeccable timing, Samuel arrived just after Saul had done the deed, a deed they both knew should have been performed by Samuel alone. Saul's disobedience was more serious than it looked, for he was challenging Samuel's spiritual authority and therefore that of the Lord, whose prophet Samuel was.

Saul was under enormous pressure and could see no escape. If he had prayed to the Lord, which he admitted to Samuel he had not, he would have found relief from his anxiety and renewal of faith. But in the midst of anxiety he acted impulsively and intruded into the prerogative of Samuel. In a moment of great strain, Saul failed to be obedient to the Lord. The penalty from Samuel was severe: "your kingdom will not endure."

It is hard to understand why Samuel, God's mouthpiece, was so tough on Saul. We will have to see the story unfold and watch the choices Saul makes in order to understand the reason for such a harsh

verdict. Samuel wanted to establish once and for all the essential difference between Israel's monarchy and that of all other nations. In
Israel the Lord was King, and obedience to him had to come first. Any
sign of an independent streak, any action that refused to take God's
instructions seriously, was tantamount to rebellion. Therefore, Samuel
said the throne would eventually be given to another, the one "after
God's own heart." Despite the terrible prophecy, Saul's remaining six
hundred men defeated the Philistines under the initiative and leadership of his son, Jonathan. Tragically, however, Saul did not learn from
this experience.

SAUL'S SECOND FAILURE (1 SAMUEL 15)

In another incident, God instructed Saul through Samuel to destroy
Israel's ancient foe, the Amalekites, along with all their livestock. But
after the battle, Saul took some Amalekite livestock as plunder and
kept their king, Agag, alive. When Samuel challenged Saul over his disobedience to God's clear directions, Saul finally admitted he did it
because of his desire to curry favor with his men, who had wanted
some material gain from the battle. But the Lord could not overlook
the persistent, deliberate rejection of his will.

What God required from Saul was obedience. No religious cere-
mony could make up for a rebellious attitude toward God and his
commandments, because it exalted self-will over divine will. Twice was
enough, and a grieving Samuel told Saul, "The Lord has torn the kingdom of Israel from you today and has given it to one of your neighbors—to one better than you."

Israel was to be distinct from other nations in that her absolute
allegiance and obedience was to God as King. If Israel's king couldn't
get that straight, what hope was there for the people?

Saul was not told how long he had left to rule, nor who his replacement would be, only that his "retirement" was now a certainty. The
identity of the next king was a carefully guarded secret that only
Samuel, the narrator, and ultimately the reader recognize.
Unbeknownst to Saul, the Lord had already secretly anointed David
to be next in line. Had Saul known that David would be king, he

would never have allowed his men to summon David to court. David was brought to court to play the harp to soothe the king's increasingly troubled spirit. Yet even without being informed of who his replacement was, Saul began to be deeply envious of David.

ENVY ENTERS (1 SAMUEL 18)

How did Saul's descent into envy develop? The problem began, in of all the unlikely places, at a party. It was time to celebrate. The triumph over the Philistines belonged both to Saul, as the commander, and to David, as the warrior who defeated Goliath. There was no reason to imagine tension or competition.

There was singing and dancing with "joyful songs and with tambourines and lutes." The women created a new song for the occasion. Saul, the song went, killed "thousands" and David killed "his tens of thousands," which in the Hebrew vernacular of the day probably meant: "Wow, did they ever kill *a lot* of those Philistine guys!" The last thing the women intended was a destructive comparison. There was more than enough joy and credit for everyone to share.

But Saul didn't hear it that way. Their innocent phrase set him off. "Saul was very angry; this refrain galled him. 'They have credited David with tens of thousands,' he thought, 'but me, with only thousands. What more can he get but the kingdom?' And from that time on Saul kept a jealous eye on David." (1 Sam. 18:8-9) Why? Because for the first time Saul began to interpret reality through the prism of envy. Maybe it was because he was not used to sharing the limelight, but Saul perceived David as a threat and a competitor from this point on.

Hearing the women sing put Saul in such a fitful state that he called upon David the very next day to play the harp in order to soothe his deeply troubled spirit. Think of the humiliation for Saul! David was the only one who could comfort him, and yet the source of Saul's discomfort was none other than *David*. David drove Saul wild, but only David could soothe him. By soothing him, David—without knowing it—only enraged Saul more! It was an impossible situation. Twice during their "music therapy" session, Saul hurled a spear at David, intending to kill him. We are not told what David thought. Maybe he just chalked it off to a royal bad hair day. But the tension was more than Saul could bear. So he removed David from court under the pretext of giving him a new assignment: to lead troops against the Philistines. Clearly his hope was that David would be eliminated.

But Saul's plan worked exactly contrary to his hope. David, of course, had only victories in the field, which made him more public and more popular than ever—and more of a problem to Saul. If Saul had checked in with the resident village psychotherapist at this point, he might have said, "I dunno, Doc, I seem to have this issue with anger, like when I go to parties and rage when the women sing. I get in these really foul moods, and then when David plays the harp, I start throwing spears at him. What's my problem?"

The problem was envy. What cannot escape our attention is the utter destructiveness of envy. It seems to devour its carrier. Some sins at least have some "buzz" to them, some deceptive yet temporary pleasure, be it ever so short-lived. But not envy. It is the one sin that offers absolutely no pleasure to its victim. Saul proved that, as we shall see.

After David's success on the battlefield, Saul's next strategy was to marry him to his eldest daughter, Merab. The proposed marriage was merely another indirect ploy to endanger David by sending him again into battle. "I won't raise a hand against him. Let the Philistines do that." For a reason we are not told, Saul offered and withdrew his daughter's hand in marriage. Perhaps it reflected Saul's instability and inability to think clearly in his rage. Never mind what his daughter felt about it.

When Saul was told that his other daughter, Michal, loved David, he was pleased. Why? "I will give her to him so she may be a snare to him and so the hand of the Philistines may be against him." Besides the shocking callousness towards his daughter's feelings, we are seeing only the beginning of Saul's obsessiveness. Saul sent a message to David assuring him that he was not to worry about being from humble origins and not having a proper dowry. Not at all! "Just be brave and go into battle, and while you're at it, would you mind bringing back a mere hundred foreskins of the Philistines?" There is no hint that

David ever questioned Saul's motive for asking him to take such a great risk. Characteristically, David was innocent, eager, and brave.

Saul must have thought, "At last, now I've got him!" And yet, David reappeared in court—ahead of the deadline—with *two* hundred foreskins. If such malice and tragic pathos did not lurk underneath the surface of this story, it would almost read like a darkly comic melodrama. David as Dudley Doright, always saving the day. And Saul, playing the dastardly villain. One can almost hear him shout, "Curses! Foiled again!" as he fingers his handlebar moustache.

But Saul kept his word and gave his daughter in marriage to a man he tried to destroy. Now David was to become his son-in-law, with entitlement to power. Knowing what we know, we can't help but wish to have been a mouse in the corner at the wedding. It would have been worth the price of the ticket just to hear Saul give the wedding toast! The point is, even Saul's determination to have his way could not overturn the loving but relentless will of God. Try as he might to destroy David, his every effort served only to enhance David. He sent David out to the fields to be destroyed, and instead David was so victorious that "all Judah and Israel loved him." He charged David to kill one hundred Philistines and he killed two hundred. Women sang songs, the people adored him, and Saul's daughter was in love with him. Saul's own son, Jonathan, was devoted to David. We see Saul increasingly more isolated, desperate, and hopeless.

After the wedding Saul could no longer hide his animosity, and he no longer cared who knew. He made it clear he intended to kill David, and the foul stench of his once-private envy was now made public. But David had strong advocates. First there was Jonathan, who at great personal risk went to his father and argued powerfully in defense of David. Saul was, in fact, persuaded and resolved not to harm him. But his resolve was short-lived, for David had yet another victory over the Philistines. Any other king would have been delighted, because the military victory was clearly in Israel's best interests. But Saul was so intensely jealous of any positive attention David received that he could feel nothing but consuming rage.

When David played the harp after the victory, Saul, who always seemed to have a spear in his hand, tried to "pin David to the wall." David escaped and fled home to his wife, Michal. She engineered David's escape by letting him out through a window to avoid the guards Saul had posted at the door to kill him.

When Saul heard that David had escaped and found refuge with Samuel, he sent his men to kill him on three separate occasions. But each time his hired guns approached, something strikingly supernatural occurred: the Spirit of God seized them so powerfully that they fell to the ground and began to prophesy, rendering them incapable of murdering David. The text gives no explanation as to the nature of these prophecies, but the experience left each man conquered by God's Spirit. Saul, in utter exasperation, set out to take care of David himself, only to have the exact same experience! Our last picture of Saul at the end of chapter 19 is of a king stripped of his robes, lying on the ground, and rendered powerless. It wasn't Saul's power that laid him out flat; it was God's power overruling his rebellion. This once-gifted leader had become an empty shell of hate. It is painful and embarrassing to watch.

It is interesting to note that the only other reference to God's Spirit in this chapter has to do with Saul's spear-throwing episodes. Each time the narrator informs us that what contributed to Saul's foul mood, besides his envy and rebellion, was an "evil spirit" dispatched from God. No evil spirit has its origin in God, but the narrator seems to want us to understand how sovereign the Lord's domain is, for even evil spirits are subject to his control and may operate only within divinely determined boundaries. God evidently held these tormenting evil spirits in check until Saul deliberately and continually chose to disobey. Thus we sense that while God prospers those who obey and love him, he allows those who oppose what is "the good and the acceptable will of the Lord" to accomplish increasingly foolish and self-destructive acts.

SAUL'S REAL PROBLEM

What a remarkable irony that Saul's pathological fear and envy targeted the one whom God had chosen as his replacement. Saul's suspicion and God's grand intent converged in David's destiny. Yet the old adage that a little knowledge is a dangerous thing really applies to Saul.

For though Saul strongly suspected that David would be his replacement, he really understood next to nothing.

Because Saul turned a blind eye to his own sin and refused to repent, he interpreted everything through his own dark lens of fear and envy. He conned himself into believing that all his problems were instigated by a power-hungry, ambitious David. But Saul should have known enough about the Lord to know that his fate could not possibly be determined by a new golden boy on the block. Even if David was the most ruthless, ambitious interloper to have ever graced this planet, it would not have mattered one whit—so long as God did not intend for him to be on the throne. For "promotion comes neither from the east nor from the west, [but] from the Lord."

Saul was the proverbial fool because he never asked the single question that ultimately matters: What is the will of Yahweh? If David truly was the Lord's choice to be the next king, Saul should have moved quickly to get his will in alignment with God's. But Saul never asked that question. Instead, he decided to get rid of his supposed enemy through a careful, devious strategy. But Saul had a far more formidable foe than he realized; he was up against the powerful resolve of Yahweh.

Saul's problem was not that David was ambitious, but rather, that David was destined. The poignant irony of the story is watching the utter futility of a man in a position of such power trying desperately to avoid what the reader knows is an assured outcome. The harder Saul tried to destroy David, the more he enabled David to succeed.

WHO NEEDS TV?

No television soap opera holds a candle to this drama! We see Israel's first king descending towards madness, the God-ordained future king dodging spears and crawling out windows, the king's son and daughter using noble and deceitful means to protect David from their father, and Saul's hit men—no better than thugs on a murder contract—suddenly falling flat on their collective faces prophesying to God. And God uses all of it, *all of it,* to accomplish his purposes. Any thought that God is so tidy as to be above using unconventional means to advance his kingdom clearly needs to be reconsidered! Hollywood agents would have been all over these people had the story happened today.

In every paragraph our text shows Saul becoming more pathetic, more evil, and, ironically, weaker in his willfulness. Saul's ultimate purposes were never accomplished, but it is chilling to see how much destruction one man caused. His obsession with David cost him a son and a daughter, and finally he lost himself. The nature of Saul's problem was complex, but it began with the sin of envy. However, we should not think of Saul's problem as merely an ancient malady; it is a very modern one as well.

THE DESCENT INTO ENVY

A collegiate friend of mine (whom I will call Anne) had a close friendship with a delightful woman her age (I will call her Molly). Anne and Molly shared the same interests and were both committed Christians. They even looked alike. But their friendship began to erode when Anne started to compare herself to Molly. Anne said, "Molly's more spiritual than I am. She's smarter and gets better grades. People respond more warmly to her than they do to me." What began as casual thoughts along these lines gradually became consuming envy, causing Anne to feel sorry for herself and hostile towards her friend.

Her own unfavorable comparisons to Molly made Anne depressed and dejected. She felt constantly diminished in her presence. Molly, sensing something was wrong, tried to praise and affirm Anne's virtues all the more. But that merely caused Anne to feel worse. Soon Anne's dejection turned to resentment and anger. *Why do I have to feel so inadequate next to her?* she asked herself. *It's just not fair!* Before long, she was using her deep self-pity to justify her envy.

Anne became obsessed with finding Molly's faults, minimizing her virtues, and calling attention to her weaknesses. She tried to make Molly's genuine piety look phony to her friends. St. Basil once described this kind of behavior with penetrating insight: "Envious persons are skilled in making what is praiseworthy seem despicable by means of unflattering distortions. . . . the envious avert their gaze from the brightness in life and the loftiness of good actions and fix their attention on rottenness." (*Concerning Envy,* Homily II)

Anne hated what she was doing, yet her failure to control her envious thoughts caused a cherished relationship to deteriorate and finally to sever. Once Anne called Molly and said, "I want to discuss the problem in our relationship." With maturity and discernment Molly answered, "Anne, there is no problem in our relationship on my end. It's you who has the problem. I think we need a cooling off period so you can sort things out in your own mind. I love you, but I can't fix what's wrong. Only you can do that. But I'll be here when you work it out."

By the time Anne came to me, she had indeed sorted through a great deal and wanted to restore her friendship with Molly. She was deeply repentant that her envy had made her behave so destructively towards Molly. And she was appalled by the damage that her envy had caused. Anne realized that the good favor Molly had with people was well-deserved, and that it was unfair to be resentful of it. She realized how obsessed and nasty she had become through her envy, and she saw how much she devalued her *own* gifts. In effect, she had been ungrateful for the blessings God had given her. Lastly, Anne came to understand that she was a highly competitive, ambitious person with a deep need to be recognized—which made her especially vulnerable to the sin of envy. She decided to contact the people to whom she had maligned Molly, and at least set the record straight by confessing her own sin. Clearly, Anne was on the way to wholeness and spiritual health. Though thankfully she stopped the process by repenting, Anne models for us both the nature and the stages of envy.

The ancients not only rank envy as one of the seven deadly sins, it is so serious as to be listed second only to pride. Because in modern times so little attention is given to its nature or stages, we need to examine both all the more carefully.

WHAT IS ENVY?

Envy rears its head when we are unable to celebrate the gifts or good fortune of another. Thomas Aquinas calls it "sorrow at another's good." Envy is the pain we feel when we perceive that someone possesses some object, quality, or status we do not possess. Why is it so painful? It is painful because when we compare ourselves unfavorably to whomever we envy, our view of ourselves is impugned. In response to the pain of the comparison that we feel diminishes us, envy seeks to bring down or destroy the one we envy.

STAGE 1: MAKING COMPARISONS

The first stage of envy always begins with comparison. Indeed, it would be hard to imagine envy taking root on a planet with only one person. Envy takes two.

Comparison may not always be inherently wrong. But since envy draws much of its poison from our feelings of inadequacy, we need to ask ourselves how we measure our worth. The Bible teaches that our worth is not determined by the things that are external—only by whether or not we have a "heart for God." If we do have a heart for God, this will be reflected in our spiritual and moral virtues. If we choose to compare ourselves with others, it should be only on these values. To make comparisons on the basis of anything else is wrong, and ultimately harmful.

However, it is not envy to look up to another person who models spiritual and moral virtues. To admire a person's courage, or faith, or loving nature can be beneficial and even laudatory. But this sort of regard must not get turned inside-out and become the breeding ground of envy. It should always remain a starting point, a place from which to begin to improve *ourselves*.

It is said that the sin of pride characteristically comes from the stance of superiority—of looking down on others. The irony of envy is that it begins by "looking up." It starts from a posture of assumed inferiority, with the "have nots" determined to cut the "haves" down to size. In essence, envy looks from below and says, "I want to be up there like you, and I resent that there is this difference. In order to rectify this great injustice, and to prevent you from making me feel inadequate, I will have to bring you down. If I can't be up there where you are right now, then you can't be there either." Dorothy Sayers wrote, "envy begins by asking plausibly: 'Why should I not enjoy what others enjoy?' and it ends by demanding: 'Why should others enjoy what I may not?'" (*The Other Six Deadly Sins*)

Even an avowed enemy's misfortune can be a threat, because what if that person gets more sympathy than I did in my misfortune? With envy, all the experiences of life, even the good ones, become a litmus test of whether an injustice has been done to the one who is envious.

Because of envy, the elder brother in the story of the Prodigal Son couldn't celebrate his brother's miraculous return by coming to the welcome-home party. "You never gave a party like that for me!" Never mind that everything his father owned was already his. Envy was shouting, "No! I've been deprived. I got a raw deal, and I bitterly resent that my brother got preferential treatment."

The elder brother clearly illustrates how blind the envious are. They are blind to God's blessings in their lives, which makes them ungrateful, and they are blind to their own sin, which makes them self-righteous and proud. In the end, the cry and final logic of the envious is always, "I've been treated unjustly and somebody owes me!" It's a miserable way to live.

STAGE 2: DEJECTION AND DEPRESSION

If the first stage of envy is making destructive comparisons, the second stage is feeling dejection and depression. We see this in Cain. Remember how his face fell in dejection because God accepted his brother Abel's gift but not his own? Of course, Cain never dealt with the fact that the Lord's preference for Abel's offering was justified because Abel offered the *choicest* of his flock, rather than "whatever was available" as Cain did.

Our dejection comes from the fact that we regard the good of another as not only diminishing us but as disgracing us. When actor John Gielgud was once asked how he defined envy, he responded with remarkable candor about his reaction to a fellow actor's good reviews: "When Sir Laurence Olivier played Hamlet in 1948, and the critics raved, I wept."

The dangerous part of this stage of envy is how often these feelings of inadequacy are soaked with self-pity. "They only credited me with thousands," whined Saul. Our self-pity makes us feel justified in nursing our wounded ego, because secretly we know that *it's just not fair*. Why must *I* feel so inadequate next to *her;* why does *he* have so much success and *I* don't? Underneath our self-pity lies a passive but powerful rage.

STAGE 3: A DESIRE TO HARM

The inevitable third stage of unchecked envy is the resentment and bitterness that boils over into the attempt to willfully harm the person making us feel inadequate. The envious may cry, "Woe is me, nobody knows the trouble I've seen," but the people we envy we also judge without mercy. Envy tries to level what it cannot imitate.

The ways of showing resentment and bitterness are endless, including backbiting, gossip, slander—anything that will prove to the world that those we envy aren't really so special, and in fact, are much worse than people suspect. Like Saul, we project onto those we envy our own evil motives and distorted perceptions of reality, and we do all of this in order to convince ourselves we are utterly justified in destroying them.

STAGE 4: IRRATIONALITY

Finally, envy, like all sin, ultimately is both irrational and "crazy-making." One day I praised a friend's great musical ability to my children. My son David, then eight years old, said, "Mom, you shouldn't say all of those nice things, because that might make us feel bad since we're just learning how to play piano."

"But, David," I protested, "that means everybody has to be exactly alike in order for us to feel good. Think how boring it would be if we were all alike. Why not just accept the fact that we aren't all equal in gifts and abilities?"

"Yeah, but what if I meet someone who can do it better than me?" he asked.

"Oh, David, you'll always meet someone who can do something better than you. So how should you respond when that happens?"

He then answered hopefully, "Pretend I'm just as good as they are anyway?"

I asked David, "Why not thank God for *their* gift and let them inspire *you* to be better?"

Yet David, with a child's honesty, got to the core of things. Envy can't celebrate a person's gifts because envy never sees people—only comparisons.

My son helped me understand something about the nature of this vice: *Envy is the great equalizer;* it hates the person for having what it does not possess. No one can be more attractive, richer, more spiritual, or more gifted than we are, because that might make us feel inadequate. That is why envy is so "crazy-making," because even a cursory glance around proves that we are not identical.

We are certainly of equal worth and value, but we are not equal in ability. To seek to make equals out of nonequals will push anyone over the edge. We may live in a country that espouses equal rights, but that doesn't make us identically gifted. In the book *The Seven Deadly Sins*, Henry Fairlie writes that because we live in an envious age, there is a widespread assumption that "everyone should be able to do and experience and enjoy everything that everyone else can do and experience and enjoy." Envy seeks to make everyone magically equal, which only pits unequals against unequals as if they are equals.

THE SIN BEHIND THE SIN

There is something even deeper about the sin of envy: It is clear that to be envious is to be improperly related towards the neighbor we are called to love. And being improperly related to our neighbor necessarily means that we are also improperly related to God. Think about it.

How much of our envy comes from struggling over things that cannot be changed? Can we change our basic intelligence, looks, gifts, social background, or biological origins with the accompanying family dysfunctions? Of course not. With whom then are we *really* angry when we succumb to envy? The truth is, our real dispute is with God, our Creator. After all, he's the one who determined or allowed those very things that we now resent.

The "sin behind the sin" of envy is that we are at swords with the Master of the Universe. We don't agree with how he dished out the goods. We don't think his wisdom has proved all that wise, and basically we don't think he's been fair. We are profoundly dissatisfied with our lot in life, and not only do we blame God for it, but we are angry with him even for allowing it. Behind our anger lies a powerful pride, insisting that we are right and God is wrong. That may not be a pretty truth to face, but at least when we face it we're getting closer to the core of the problem.

There are some famous examples that prove this to be so. Why didn't the elder brother in the parable of the Prodigal Son go to the party? Only partly because he was envious of his brother getting the VIP treatment. Ultimately, it was because he was *furious* with his *father*. He disagreed with his father's judgment. His father had been too lavish and overly forgiving. Revenge was required—not forgiveness!

Peter Shaffer's play *Amadeus* deals brilliantly with the theme of envy. In it we see the struggle of Salieri, a court musician of average skill but one who aspired to musical greatness. He recognized the genius of Mozart, and his envy of Mozart consumed him. Shaffer not only helps us understand the nature of envy, but he reveals the metaphysical problem when he ties envy to questions about the justice of how God distributes gifts.

What outrages Salieri is that God would give such a sublime gift to a man like Mozart, this "giggling child . . . this spiteful, sniggering, conceited, infantine Mozart." But even worse, argues Salieri, God put into his own heart the *longing* to create sublime music and the *ability* to discern greatness, but without the gift to produce it. "You put into me the perception of the Incomparable, which most men never know! Then you ensured that I would know myself forever mediocre."

The envious often hide behind an outward sense of duty when in fact this sense of duty really is a cover for the manipulation and control of those they envy. "Until this day I pursued virtue with rigor. I have labored long hours to relieve my fellow men. I have worked and worked the talent you allowed me. You know how hard I worked! Solely that in the end . . . I might hear your voice! And now I do hear it, and it says only one name: Mozart!"

Salieri fully admits his envy and his insight is quite rare, for he knows that he is really at odds with God alone. What is to be done since he is the sole man alive who clearly recognizes God's gift to Mozart? The solution is clear: Salieri declares war against God. "From this time we are enemies, you and I! I'll not accept it from you, do you hear? They say God is not mocked. I tell you, *Man* is not mocked! . . . They say the Spirit bloweth where it listeth: I tell you No! . . . you are the Enemy! . . . And this I swear: To my last breath I shall block you on earth, as far as I am able!" Salieri's ultimate act of revenge against God is to slit his own throat, not out of sorrow or repentance, but rather as a final act of autonomous rebellion against God.

Perhaps Salieri sounds extreme, but he brilliantly exposes the sin behind envy. We are angry with how God runs his universe. We don't agree with his judgments or accept his sovereignty. We think we got a raw deal and God is to blame.

THE WOUND BEHIND THE SIN

If Saul's life teaches us anything, it's that the sin of envy wounds us psychologically as well. We all have some emotional deficits—"holes in the soul"—usually resulting from fundamental needs that were never met. That does not excuse sin, but it does enable us to understand why we are vulnerable to certain temptations.

Is there an emotional wound that would make us especially vulnerable to the sin of envy? Leanne Payne writes in *Listening Prayer* that envy is often rooted in the excruciating pain of feeling deserted, or the intense fear of abandonment. If that is true, then Saul is a textbook case, for his continuing kingship had been rejected by God. But who was responsible for the Lord's negative response to Saul? Saul himself was to blame, as we have seen. But Saul had a choice. He could take responsibility for his past failure and turn to God, asking how he could help the next in line, or he could refuse to accept God's verdict and fight back. Tragically, he chose the latter course.

THE PERSONAL HARM BEHIND THE SIN

What makes envy so very deadly? Saul clearly shows us that besides the horrific damage it does to others, envy does even worse to its carrier. It torments. It leaves us addicted to and obsessed with our target and yet offers no pleasure. It destroys relationships and causes us to live by comparison, constantly looking sideways at the object of our envy rather than rejoicing and looking upwards to God. It makes us bitter, resentful people, always complaining that our glass is half-empty. Finally, it leaves us in isolation. Envy is so self-destructive that those consumed by it are willing to suffer great injury so long as those they envy suffer even more.

WHAT TO DO ABOUT ENVY

What can deliver us from this bondage? What things can we do to overcome envy?

Repent

First, as with all the vices, we must call envy what it is—a horrible, destructive sin. We must confess it as such, and then decide we will not continue to do it. That may sound simplistic or naive, or even impossible, but it is the first step. Until we exercise our human will—that dimension of our being enabling us to choose God over self—and accept responsibility for our conscious decision to sin, we won't get to first base.

But God's response to our confessions—and the character deficits they reveal—is always the same. No matter where we are, or who we are, or what we have done, God's heart is always open to us. "Love surrounds us, seeking the smallest crack by which it may rush in," George MacDonald has written. In *The Song of a Passionate Heart*, David Roper writes, "We are not what he wants us to be, but we are not unwanted. If we will have him, he will be our shepherd." God is exceedingly sympathetic to emotional woundedness that makes us susceptible to sin. Indeed, his intention is to "heal the brokenhearted and bind up their wounds."

Actually, it is because of God's compassion that he insists we deal firmly with sin before it destroys us and others. It is most often only after the moral act of repentance that God begins to heal the emotional problems underlying the spiritual ones. Thus, while God "knows our frame and remembers that we are but dust," he still expects us to own up to our troubles. We must not insist on being healed before we obey him; we need only respond to God's clear commands. When we do, he will strengthen us to overcome.

Live the Truth

Like every sin, envy always involves deception. It exaggerates the value of another and diminishes our own value. We must stop giving the one we envy so much power! When we are tempted to envy, we should ask, Can this person heal me if I get cancer? Can she forgive my sins? Will he be the one to judge my life when I die? Why am I investing so much needless energy comparing myself to other finite human beings?

Furthermore, do we really know enough about another person's life to be truly envious? I once heard a friend say to another friend, "You know, I used to feel a little envious of you. I wanted to be well known and professionally successful like you. But now that I've seen the inside track and know what it's taken to become godly, it's solved my problem of envy!" The truth is, no one's life is as it appears. We all have our own unique pressure and pain and baggage. It is foolish to want to be someone else, for all it means is exchanging our set of problems for theirs.

Count Your Blessings

We need to live in truth, which involves thanking God again and again for the many gifts and blessings he has given us. But when we're feeling envious we often fail to recognize what comes from the hand of God.

One evening I had friends over for a "house blessing." It had been a delightful evening of prayer and singing, going from one room to the next to dedicate the entire house. Later, as I was tucking my children into bed, my daughter suddenly burst into tears. I was flabbergasted and asked what was wrong. Evidently, everyone had prayed *four* prayers in her brother's bedroom, and only *one* prayer in hers. I comforted her, but I knew this was also an opportunity. I asked her, "How are you feeling right now, Elizabeth?"

"Awful!"

"Do you feel like you missed out on the fun of the party?" I asked.

"Yes!" she responded angrily.

"Did you know there is a word for what you are feeling right now?" She looked puzzled but intrigued. "It's called envy, and you have really told the truth about envy. It makes us feel miserable and *always* causes us to miss out on the party."

"Well, how do you get rid of it?" she asked.

"That is a very wise question. You recently served food to the homeless. How do you think a homeless person would feel to hear what you are saying?"

With lightning speed she said, "They would say I was lucky to even have a home. They'd say they wished they even had a bed to sleep in. Oh, Mom, I'm sorry. Now what do you call that thing I was feeling again?" she asked softly.

"It's called envy, and I think you just got rid of it," I answered.

Conquering envy requires us to see it for what it is—a dissatisfaction and lack of contentment with life, leading to anger with God. What lies behind our anger is ingratitude and horrible pride. In our self-righteous envy we feel we have permission, even justification, to punish our neighbor for having been given what we perceive as favorable treatment. But envy always backfires; it hurts the one we envy and ultimately devours us.

QUESTIONS AND REFLECTIONS

1. Whom do you envy? What makes you feel inferior to someone else?

2. Review the stages of envy. Where are you in your struggle? Brainstorm ideas for pulling out of each stage.

3. What is the source of your envy? Does it come from pride, or falsely thinking you are superior to others? (You cannot tolerate that others should possess something you don't.) Does it come from despondency, or falsely thinking you are of lesser worth than others? (You feel sorry for yourself and search for ways to reduce the deficiencies you perceive.)

4. Reconsider the underlying assumptions you have about what makes you a worthy individual. Think about it from God's perspective. See 1 Samuel 13:14; Micah 6:8; Galatians 5:22; and Philippians 3:8-9.

5. Reflect upon the danger of what your envy is doing to you. What kind of person did Saul become through his envy? What fruit do you see in your life that envy produces (focusing on the negative, being judgmental and critical, minimizing a person's virtues and positive achievements, bitterness)?

Chapter
Four

Compassion:
The Remedy for Envy

God has not created us to live life negatively, with our focus on beating down what is wrong. He calls us, instead, to rejoice and to think on those things that are true and excellent of nature. We are to lift up our souls to what is good. Therefore, one of the most powerful remedies in defeating a vice is to focus attention on developing a virtue! The best way to conquer the vice of envy is to develop the virtue of compassion.

Compassion is having an intense, heartfelt empathy for others. It is the ability to put ourselves in someone else's shoes. The Scriptures remind us to "weep with those who weep and rejoice with those who rejoice." If envy weeps at those who celebrate and celebrates with those who weep, true compassion sees another's sorrow and wants to help. It looks at another's success and wants to praise.

IT STARTS WITH GOD

Like all human virtues, compassion draws its source from God: "His compassion is over all that he has made." (Ps. 145:9) When a leper came to Jesus, desperate to be healed, and said, "If you are willing, I know you could heal me," the Gospel writer Mark tells us that Jesus' heart was "filled with compassion and he reached out and touched him saying, 'I will. Be healed.'" Once Jesus saw a huge crowd gathered, and they were eager for him to teach. He was "moved with compassion," because they looked to him like "sheep without a shepherd." When the Lord saw a widow whose only son had died, "his heart went out to her, and he said, 'Don't cry.'"

Compassion is not something awarded only to the deserving or the righteous; it flows from the heart of God to all. When the Pharisees wanted to frighten Jesus into leaving their area, they told him that Herod wanted to kill him. Jesus cried out: "O Jerusalem, Jerusalem, you who kill the prophets and stone those sent to you, how often I have longed to gather your children together, as a hen gathers her chicks under her wings, but you were not willing!" (Luke 13:34) That is the nature of compassion.

In Colossians 3:12, Paul tells us that Christians are to "put on heartfelt compassion." Jesus tells us to "be merciful as your Father in heaven is merciful." (Luke 6:36) Christians are also especially charged to be compassionate to the needy, to those in distress, to the fatherless, the widowed and the orphan.

As I seek to raise my children to be loving, I often ask myself what makes a person kind. We live in such a mean-spirited age, where we are so quick to be harsh and judgmental. Yet there is little evidence to suggest that the Christian community is any different. But we *should* be different!

My good friend Doug Calhoon recently told me a story. He has always been a fitness buff, and has gone to a gym for the last twelve years to work out. In all that time, he never saw people reach out to each other in friendship. Few even knew each other's names, for they were there for one purpose—to compete. The atmosphere was charged with beating the other guy in racquetball or tennis, or lifting more weights than the next guy.

But Doug received a very serious injury, and instead of frequenting the gym, he had to go to a rehabilitation center designed for people with physical injuries. He was astounded by the difference in atmosphere between the two places. Within two days at the rehab center, everyone knew his name. Instead of worrying about being out-done, the people there encouraged him. All he heard were comments like, "Hey, good job!" or, "Way to go!" It suddenly dawned on Doug that he was being cheered on with every incremental bit of success and improvement he charted.

In the gym there was no room for anything less than perfection. One's neighbor served only as a competitor, and failure or weakness was disdained. But in the rehabilitation center it was understood that you wouldn't be there unless you were broken and needed healing. And your brokenness wasn't a source of shame. Instead, the empha-sis was "You have come to the right place. *We are with you every step of the way.* Any growth, no matter how small, is a cause for celebra-tion!" Then Doug commented, "Which place do you think the church ought to be like? How often have people's experience been more like the gym than the rehab center?"

God's compassion flows out of his steadfast refusal to give up on his wayward children. His kindness and tender mercies are abundant despite our unworthiness and defects. So if God, who is altogether per-fect, is still loving and compassionate to sinners, why are we, who are sinful and in constant need of forgiveness, not merciful and compas-sionate as well?

How do we "put on" compassion and teach our children to do the same? We need role models who embody the virtue of compassion. Role models like Saul's son, Jonathan.

JONATHAN: THE PICTURE OF COMPASSION

When David returned triumphant after his single-handed defeat of Goliath, Jonathan could easily have been the one most envious. After all, Jonathan was the heir-apparent. However, he not only celebrated David's victory, but in an act of spontaneous abandonment he took off his robe, tunic, sword, belt, and bow, and gave them to David! Perhaps he didn't want David going to court too humbly dressed. Yet the act could have been perceived as Jonathan signifying that David might take his place as successor to the throne. It was an unexpected, extra-ordinarily selfless act.

So selfless, in fact, that we can only imagine Jonathan's business manager rushing over afterwards and saying, "Ah, *real* bad career move there, Jonathan. But never mind. Tomorrow we'll do some damage control, and here's the spin we'll use: 'Due to the excitement of the moment and the extreme heat at that time of the day, Jonathan, the future king, while deeply grateful for David's bravery in battle, wishes to clarify that his gifts to David were merely a token of Jonathan's own generous nature. He wants to take this opportunity to thank David for making Israel and the throne a safer place from which *Jonathan* will eventually rule.'"

That would be the expected human response of an heir-apparent. But Jonathan never seemed to pay any thought to himself, or what was good for his career. Why did he extend such an extravagant gesture? Why didn't he worry more about how David's popularity might impact his career? The reason was, as the narrator tells us, that Jonathan felt "one in spirit" with David and he "loved him as himself." That is envy's opposite, not to be in competition "against," but in solidarity "with." When love is expressed through compassion, it is simply incompatible with envy. The two do not exist simultaneously.

But compassion for one's neighbor goes beyond "rejoicing with those who rejoice." It also involves "weeping with those who weep." When David's life was in danger because of Saul's murderous intent, Jonathan, at enormous personal risk, tried to dissuade his father. He knew Saul might consider him disloyal, perhaps even a traitor to Israel's throne. Yet Jonathan reasoned carefully with his father on David's behalf, in spite of the great danger. David's troubles became Jonathan's troubles. There wasn't an ounce of competition or self-interest on Jonathan's part—only heartfelt compassion for David's plight and a desire to help his friend.

How was such a response possible? What frees us to rejoice and weep with others without the horrible self-preoccupation that tormented King Saul? What was behind Jonathan's love for David that allowed him to be so compassionate?

THE ROOTS OF COMPASSION

Seeing Ourselves Accurately Before God

The more we read about Jonathan, the more we realize how extraordinary he actually was. It's easy for us to take for granted his heroic acts on behalf of David, because we know that David was destined to be king. But Jonathan had no such knowledge of David's destiny at this point in the story. Jonathan's compassion is even more remarkable considering that he no doubt wanted very much to be the next king of Israel. But instead, he put aside his own self-interests to do what was in the best interest of David.

What enabled him to do that? Why didn't Jonathan cling to his prerogative as heir-apparent? Yes, it was due in part to his deep love for David, but that still doesn't address why he wasn't more possessive of the throne.

The answer has to be that Jonathan saw himself accurately before God. God is the Creator and Lord; Jonathan was the creature. God was in control of his destiny. Therefore, being a king wasn't a possession he could control, but a gift that only God could give. What a contrast to his father! If God was indeed in charge, Jonathan could celebrate David's victory without looking over his shoulder. Why should he worry about David's success, knowing that the Lord God was looking out for both of them?

Jonathan's life is a testimony to the freedom that comes when we see ourselves accurately before God, and when we humbly submit to his sovereignty. Now we are free to accept our neighbor's blessing without envy. For if God is sovereign, then what is it to us if he chooses to bless our neighbor with abundant gifts?

Seeing Our Sin and Our Radical Need for Grace

Although we do not see this principle quite as clearly in the story of Jonathan, we are free to be compassionate once we acknowledge that we are sinners in radical need of God's grace. It is only when we face our sin and desperate need for this grace that we are able to experience the depth of God's compassion toward us. As Francis De Sales comments in *The Introduction to the Devout Life,* we must love our abjection, our poverty, and our unworthiness, because through these things we experience God's compassion.

To experience God's mercy also dramatically affects how we see others. Once we have sampled God's love and compassion, we cannot help but extend that same leniency to others. But as Jesus makes very clear, woe unto us if we fail to be compassionate. In the parable of the unmerciful servant (Matt. 18:21-35), the Lord taught that there are serious consequences for those who lack such a spirit: "'You wicked servant, I cancelled all that debt of yours because you begged me to. Shouldn't you have had compassion on your fellow-servant, just as I had compassion on you?' In anger his master turned him over to his jailers to be tortured, until he should pay back all he owed." After this story, Jesus added these stern words: "This is how my heavenly father will treat each one of you unless you forgive your brother from your heart."

When we encounter Christians who are arrogant, judgmental, and without compassion, it is safe to conclude that they have never tasted the depth of God's mercy, because they have never faced the depths of their own sin. As Corrie ten Boom once said, "You see, I love so much . . . because I have been forgiven of so much."

THE FRUIT OF COMPASSION

We Are Set Free!

What is the fruit that a compassionate life yields? Look at the spontaneous joy and carefree abandon of Jonathan! He didn't have to worry about his future—that was God's problem. He didn't have to glance sideways to see if David was showing him up, because he knew his life would be judged, not in comparison with David, but according to his faithfulness to God.

With a compassionate spirit, we too can enter deeply into the joy and blessings of our neighbors. Even if their success happens to come at a time when our future is uncertain, or when we are in sorrow, we can still rejoice because we know we are trusting a God who has wonderful plans for us, too. God never blesses another person at our expense.

Jonathan vividly demonstrated an unrestrained freedom that came from living life compassionately. Would we rather be like Saul, so eaten up with envy that he felt he must always keep a spear at his side for fear someone would take what was his? Or Jonathan, who joyfully ripped off his royal garments and handed them over to David without counting the cost?

Free to Live for God

Once we understand that our future, our blessings, our worth, our reputation, and our success are all in the hands and under the control of a loving God, we can sit back and rest. God's plans for his children are plans of "hope and not despair." No longer do we need to pander after the praise of people. People can be for us one day and against us the next; ultimately, it doesn't even matter. It's God's judgment of our lives alone that matters.

In keeping our eyes on God and letting his commendation, "Well done thou good and faithful servant," be what we live for, envy will be curbed and compassion will be encouraged. If we are exercising our gifts and concentrating on how to serve God better, we won't have time to envy others' gifts, and the expression of our gifts can itself be a form of celebration—a living out of our gratefulness to God for his blessing.

The late Paul Tournier's wife Nellie said of her famous psychiatrist husband, "For years I lived under the shadow of Paul's brilliance and gifts. He didn't put that on me; I did that to myself by constantly comparing myself to him and feeling inadequate. Then one day I read the parable of the talents and felt the Lord say to me, 'Nell, when you get to heaven I'm not going to ask you what you did with Paul's gifts. I'm going to ask you what you did with yours.' I repented of my sin. And from that day forth I took my eyes off of Paul and began looking to God, and asking how could I use my gifts in service to him."

LIVING WITH COMPASSION

In our home we have a system. When someone puts someone down, one of us says, "Oh, oh! That was a 'put-down.' Now you have to say three 'put-ups!'" Right then, on the spot, that person has to say three positive things about the one criticized. It may sound silly, but I've been amazed at how well it has worked.

Once I told my children Elizabeth and David that they could invite friends to go bowling one Saturday afternoon. They broke up into two teams, the boys against the girls. Initially, there were gales of laughter and much fun. But it didn't take long before things started going downhill. The boys were incredibly competitive but just enough younger that they couldn't keep up with the girls, which horrified them but thrilled the girls.

Soon the carping and put-downs began. The girls were amazingly adept at humiliation: "Greeaaat gutter shot." The boys tried their best to keep up with the verbal slams, but when all else failed they just tripped the girls as they walked by. Let's just say it was one of the longest Saturdays I ever spent. I was amused when the bowling alley owner walked up and offered me a free pitcher of beer for my courage. At that moment the beer didn't sound strong enough!

As we piled into the car, I said, "You guys told me you watched the Winter Olympics. There are two important things in sports—excellence and character. For excellence in athletic skill, they give you a gold medal. But for an athlete, character, or sportsmanship, is considered just as important as skill. I'm curious, what kind of medal do you think you would have received today for the way you treated each other?" Dead silence. Then one said, "Ah, that all depends. Does slugging someone mean you don't qualify for a medal?" Then, to my surprise, they all acknowledged they hadn't been very nice. The consensus was that only Mary would get the gold medal for character, because she had been sweet to everyone.

I told the kids about our practice of "put-ups," and then I asked each boy to tell one of the girls something he appreciated about her. I asked the girls to do the same thing with the boys. I heard things like,

"Okay, I think you really have great potential, and you tried so hard"; "You are nice most of the time"; "Well, you may not be a great bowler, but I think you're a nice person." The difference this little exercise made was astonishing. Attitudes softened and smiles came on faces as the kids practiced verbalizing gratitude for each other.

Acquiring compassion, like acquiring any virtue, takes much practice. And God's grace. It does not happen overnight, but it's worth every ounce of the effort.

THE INSPIRATION OF MODELS

As important as on-the-job compassion training is, there is nothing quite as effective as the example of heroes. I have been amazed to see my son David's fascination with the Olympic runner Eric Liddell. After he watched the film *Chariots of Fire,* David could not get enough information about Eric. He has read every book he could find on the runner. Since our close friend Ruth Nyquist was with Liddell in an internment camp in China, David has riddled her with question after question about him. Sometimes David even runs with his head tossed back in the air, as Eric did. There is no mistake, Eric Liddell is one of his heroes.

But we need more than heroes of the past. One of the most effective training tools in character development is exposing ourselves and our families to people who model the type of traits we are seeking in our own lives. My very dear friends and neighbors, Jim and Ruth Nyquist, have been powerful models of compassion to me and my children. For example, they once made a promise to Jim's relative Arloween, who was more like a sister than a cousin, that they would care for her in her old age if she ever became unable to care for herself. Because Arloween and her husband, Ev, were childless, they had poured their lives into a ministry to the young. Then several years after her husband's death, 81-year-old Arloween fell and suffered several minor strokes. They brought her to their home to recuperate, and decided that the time to fulfill their promise had come. She now lives with them permanently.

When my children first met Arloween, she was frail and struggling, though the beauty of her character still shone through. However, gradually over the weeks and months, the children began to see a different person emerge. Through the enormous love and encouragement of Ruth and Jim, Arloween began to gain strength and to participate in lively discussions at the table. Her comments always reflected great wisdom and insight, and she even began to make jokes. Every time we saw her she seemed more alive, with a deeper twinkle in her eye. Even her ability to cope with short-term memory loss astounded my children. When Elizabeth asked her if she had enjoyed helping us put up the art in our home the day before, Arloween answered, "I'm sorry, I don't remember being at your house yesterday. But I have two questions for you: Did I have a good time and did I do a good job?" Of course we all roared with laughter, but later Elizabeth said, "Oh, Mom, I hope I'm that cheerful if something like that ever happens to me." Many times after being in the Nyquist home, the children would say, "Boy, Arloween is getting so much better. That's because she's being loved so well."

Once when the Nyquists were away for a week, I suggested that we go over and set up the house for a "welcome home." I braced myself for comments like, "Mother, I have homework," or "Can't I have a friend over?" There have certainly been times in the past when I suggested doing things for people and heard initial grumbling and complaining! But not this time. They could hardly wait! They cut flowers from the Nyquists' marvelous English garden, and we arranged them in every room. The children sorted their mail, wrote them cards, and helped me set the table and prepare a meal. They worked feverishly and with joy to make the homecoming special.

After we finished our labors and went from room to room to inspect our work, David said, "Mom, doesn't it make you feel good to do something kind for people like the Nyquists who help . . . oh, you know, the world?" Later, I said to Elizabeth, "The Nyquists and Arloween are going to be so happy to see how pretty everything looks. They had to leave things a bit spartan since they would be gone for a while." Elizabeth looked at me with a horrified expression and said, "Mother! How could you ever say this house is spartan when it is so full of the love of God?! You feel it the minute you walk in this door. Just look at what has happened to Arloween!"

I have never been so grateful to stand corrected in my life. In a low moment, Arloween once said, "Becky, I just wish the Lord would take me home to heaven. I don't know why I'm still here." And I answered her, "Well, I can give you two reasons why the Lord has kept you. You have no idea what your grace and courage in difficulty, and Jim and Ruth's love and compassion and generosity, have modeled to my children. If for no other reason than two little lives, I thank the Lord he has kept you."

Compassion is contagious. Let's catch it—and expose ourselves and our children to goodness every chance we get!

SUGGESTIONS TO HELP BUILD COMPASSION

1. It is our duty to love, so make a "goodness file" on the person you envy. What are the positive qualities that make him or her lovable? Speak about those virtues to someone else. Consider Philippians 2:1-4 and 4:8.

2. Develop compassion: Ask God to help you see the person you envy through his eyes. Might there be pain and suffering in the person's life about which you know nothing? Ask God to soften your heart and to help you show his love to that person.

3. Practice gratitude: Remind yourself of God's divine wisdom and goodness. Make a list of the positive and valuable things he has given you. Look at Psalm 34:1-4 and Ephesians 4:32.

4. Share your struggle with envy with a trusted Christian friend who will pray for you and hold you accountable. Naming our evil tends to rob it of its power, its grip on our hearts.

Chapter Five

Hatred:
A Consuming Fire

J esus told us to love our neighbor as ourselves. He went even further and said we are to pray for our enemies and demonstrate love
to those who seek to harm us. So what do we do when we hate
the "neighbor" we are supposed to love?

When I lived in Portland, Oregon, I heard Corrie ten Boom tell a
story that has always been to me a forceful demonstration of the power
of God's love to conquer hate. During World War II and the Nazi occupation of Holland, this remarkable Dutch woman and her family were
sent to Ravensbruck concentration camp for hiding Jews in their home.

When she came onto the stage in Portland, her opening remark
was, "I don't want you to take any notes, or listen to anything I say
unless you know who I am." The audience chuckled softly because
everyone knew who Corrie was.

Then she proceeded, "My name is Corrie ten Boom and I am a
murderer." There was total silence. "You see, when I was in prison
camp I saw the same guard day in and day out. He was the one who
mocked and sneered at us when we were stripped and taken to the
showers. We felt the shame of walking naked past this man. I could
see my sister's frail form ahead of me, ribs sharp beneath the parch-
ment of skin. He spat on us in contempt, and I hated him. I hated him
with every fiber of my being. With every evil act he committed my

hatred grew day by day. I knew that it was all right to hate evil. But I hated the sinner! Jesus says when you hate someone, you are guilty of murder. So I wanted you to know right from the start that you are listening to a murderer.

"When we were freed, I left Germany vowing never to return," Corrie continued. "But I was invited back there to speak. I did not want to go, but I felt the Lord nudging me. Very reluctantly I went. My first talk was on forgiveness. As I was speaking, I saw to my horror that same prison guard sitting in the audience. When he had last seen me, I was emaciated, sick, and my hair was shorn. I don't know if he recognized me at that point, but I could never forget his face, never. It was clear to me from the radiant look on his face while I spoke that he had been converted since I last saw him.

"After I had finished speaking, he came up to me and said with a beaming smile, 'Ah, sister Corrie, isn't it wonderful how God forgives? How good it is to know that, as you say, all our sins are at the bottom of the sea!' And he extended his hand for me to shake. It was the first time since my release that I had been face to face with one of my captors, and my blood seemed to freeze.

"All I felt as I looked at him was hate. I said to the Lord silently, 'There is nothing in me that could ever love that man. I hate him for what he did to me and to my family. But you tell us that we are supposed to love our enemies. That's impossible for me, but nothing is impossible for you. So if you expect me to love this man it's going to have to come from you, because all I feel is hate.'

"'You mentioned Ravensbruck in your talk,' he said. 'I was a guard there. But since that time,' he went on, 'I have become a Christian. I know that God has forgiven me for the cruel things I did there, but I would like to hear it from your lips as well. Fraulein—' again his hand came out—'will you forgive me?'

"Forgiveness is an act of the will, and the will can function regardless of the temperature of the heart. 'Jesus, help me!' I prayed silently. 'I can lift my hand. I can do that much. You supply the feeling.'"

She told us that at that moment she felt nudged to do only one thing: "Put out your hand, Corrie," the Lord seemed to say. Then she told us, "It took all of the years that I had quietly obeyed God in obscurity to do the hardest thing I have ever done in my life. I put out my hand." Then she said something remarkable happened. "It was only after my simple act of obedience that I felt something like warm oil was being poured over me. And with it came the unmistakable message: 'Well done, Corrie. That's how my children behave.' And the hate in my heart was absorbed and gone. And so one murderer embraced another murderer, but in the love of Christ."

Then Corrie, in her wonderful Dutch accent, said, "Yes, I am a murderer. But you are listening to one gloriously freed and forgiven murderer. You see, I love so much because I have been forgiven of so much!"

Corrie's story is unusual at certain points. Most of us have not had to face the evil and endure the pain of prison camp. Perhaps that is why God reached out to her so immediately and quickly. Yet, as I listened to her, I was struck by the thought that elements of her story are common to all of us. Corrie's initial response to the guard in prison was not hate. Hate takes time to grow and fester, but once allowed in, it is very difficult to defeat. She recognized that it was not wrong to hate evil, for indeed there would have been something seriously wrong with her had she not been outraged by the evil she experienced. But it was wrong for her to hate the one who did the evil. We also get trapped when we allow hate to focus not only on the sin but on the sinner. And, of course, hating someone is a sin. Like the person who wronged us, we now have become an offender too. If we fail to deal with our sin, it will grow and take on a life of its own. And therein lies a principle of life.

A SIN BEYOND ENVY

Everything that constitutes life exhibits a restless, creative, growing dynamic. Astronomers say that nothing in our world remains the same and that even the supposedly fixed North Star is constantly moving. Our own galaxy is itself revolving, making one revolution every two hundred million years. Change seems to be the very essence and definition of cosmic life. Nothing can be put on hold and frozen, because there is a dynamic quality to all of life. Death may be static, but life never is.

This dynamic quality also applies to evil. Once a choice has been made for good or for evil, the consequences run their course, because unrepentant sin does not remain stagnant and then disappear. Rather, it nearly always deepens and widens into something worse. If one chooses to do evil, only repentance can stop the dynamic process.

Biblical examples of the destructiveness of evil abound. When we left Saul in the last chapter, he was consumed with envy. That was bad enough. But we now discover that Saul's envy led to something much worse. It led to *hatred*, one of the most complex and binding sins of all, and probably the saddest result of envy.

Cain's problem with his brother Abel began as envy but degenerated into murderous hatred. The envy of Joseph's older brothers led to such a deep and venomous hatred that they attempted to get rid of him permanently by selling him to Egyptian traders.

But hatred is not only envy-induced. Lust also can quickly degenerate into hate, as the story of the rape of Tamar by her half-brother Amnon reveals very vividly. Overcome with desire, Amnon raped Tamar but immediately afterwards he "was filled with utter hatred for her; his hatred was stronger than the love he had felt, and he said to her servants, 'Get rid of this woman, put her out and bolt the door after her.'"

Modern evidence of this destructive progression to hatred also abounds. The results are all about us. Hate virtually permeates our culture, from the self-hatred expressed through eating disorders or drug addiction to the hate expressed through open gang warfare, racial riots, sexual abuse, or the increased murder rate. We see Americans joining white supremacist groups, parents abusing children, and school children assaulting one another and their teachers—hatred run rampant.

Is the Christian community immune? In a recent interview in *Servant Magazine*, Gordon MacDonald said, "What I see among evangelical people is not righteous anger, but *hatred*. . . . [Some Christians] spread hatred on anybody who differs from [them] on moral and ethical issues. [Consider] when we see guys shooting doctors at abortion clinics. That all this could erupt in the community that's supposed to be known for its peacemaking absolutely amazes me."

Perhaps hatred—not merely righteous indignation—is closer to the church of Christ than we want to admit. We have only to examine our own hearts to find its reactions to those who have hurt, offended, betrayed, or abused us. We have trouble forgiving; we struggle with anger, resentment, bitterness; we even hate. We find it impossible to change the feelings that storm our soul. We are trapped. How did we get to this point? We need to look again at the example of Saul to learn how one succumbs to hatred and how it can be overcome.

SAUL'S DESCENT INTO HATRED

What made Saul vulnerable to hatred in the first place? Let's be honest. It is hard for a CEO to give up power. On a plane recently, I sat next to the wife of an American corporate mogul who is a household name. We established rapport quickly, and before long she began telling me what it was like to live with someone so famous. Nothing about her life made me want to trade mine for hers. She told me of the enormous difficulty her husband was experiencing in turning over his corporation to someone younger. He was retiring by choice and with many accolades and honors. Yet he was not handling it very well; indeed, he was an emotional basket case. We have all heard what happens to people who have no other source of identity but their work. According to his wife, this man was a textbook case of someone who didn't know what to do with himself. She said, "If only he had invested some energy in developing an identity as a husband or father or a churchman. All of his energy was spent on work. Now that it's gone, so is his identity."

In the best of circumstances, it is extremely difficult for a CEO to step down. But imagine the terror that would strike you if you were fired from a job that gave you a sense of being and power and prestige. That was Saul's situation. Samuel had just given him his "termination papers," due to a negative performance evaluation from Saul's "Boss." The choice before Saul was probably the same choice that all CEOs have when their time is up. Will they behave with humility and dignity during their remaining days in office? Will they determine to face squarely the flaws that brought the termination? Will they blame the boss or even their successor for their woes? When the time comes, will they exit as statesmen, with behavior worthy of the office, or will they embarrass everyone by clinging to the last vestige of power? Being fired or asked to step aside is always traumatic.

No question, Saul was in a tough spot. We already know that he had a brooding temperament, an anxious uncertainty that made it difficult for him to act decisively as a leader must. Not knowing who his replacement would be or how many days he had left in office no doubt aggravated his condition. It would have been natural to have many conflicting feelings. If only he'd been given more time to prove himself. It seemed to him that David had gotten all the breaks. Would people remember the good things Saul had accomplished during his reign? Why was he allowed so little margin of error?

But Saul should have asked himself two pertinent questions: Was his dethronement God's will, and what sins of his had made it necessary? God's treatment of Saul is a complex subject, one that many biblical commentators have struggled over. Some commentators feel that Saul's "firing" was not fair, that he was evaluated prematurely and too severely. Some believe that Saul was dogged by a fate beyond his control, a viewpoint explored in depth by David Gunn (*The Fate of King Saul*). It is not impossible to understand this point of view. We might also wonder if Samuel's judgment was premature. If Saul had been given a bit more time, would his performance have improved? What could have transpired had he faced his sin and repented?

Yet the point is that Saul was given more time. He ruled for at least ten years beyond the time God sent Samuel to tell Saul he had been rejected by God. But over those years, we see no sign of Saul being able to take the rebuke, repent, and exercise his kingship alongside David until his time was up. Instead he stubbornly refused to admit any wrong. Even Gunn concedes that Saul contributed to his own downfall through his envy of David and his refusal to accept God's verdict. We know that as humans, we can't see into Saul's inner being and know his motivation. But God is the "heart knower," and though his judgment of Saul may seem premature to some, it was more than justified. Saul sank into deeper and deeper sin, causing inestimable and nearly irredeemable harm to innocent people because of his own rebelliousness.

Saul's life also demonstrates that sin is dynamic in nature. Because he refused to deal with it, that sin festered and grew into something much worse. That is where our story continues.

SAUL GETS PUT TO THE TEST (1 SAMUEL 20)

David experienced plenty of Saul's crazed envy. He had to dodge Saul's spears and slip past his hit men to escape the king's treachery. But had Saul's erratic impulses now turned to willful malice? David had to know if Saul really planned to kill him.

In great anguish he asked his trusted friend Jonathan, "What have I done? What is my crime? How have I wronged your father, that he is trying to take my life?" (1 Sam. 20:1) Jonathan hung on to the hope that his father had not sunk to such a low level. David, however, feared the worst, for he had experienced Saul's mood swings and unpredictability firsthand. So the men devised a test to determine Saul's true intent toward David.

David decided to miss the royal dinner at the New Moon Festival celebration. This was a religious feast at which David should have been present, for there was an assigned seat for him. David would be conspicuously absent. Jonathan would offer a plausible excuse, claiming that David wanted to participate in an annual sacrifice with his family in Bethlehem. How Saul handled the news would reveal his intentions. If Saul became angry, presumably he intended to use the occasion to kill David.

Life tests our character whether we want it to or not. Some intriguing stories in biblical literature tell of tests intentionally set up to determine someone's character. Joseph devised a test to see if his mean-spirited brothers had really changed. David and Jonathan carried out a similar test, but theirs was no case of entrapment. There was no sense of gleeful anticipation to see if their fears were substantiated. "Ah-hah, just as we suspected!" Indeed, Jonathan was still not only reluctant to believe that his father harbored such malice, but apparently was completely ignorant of Saul's clear intention to kill David. David hoped his own suspicions were unfounded, although he believed the chances of this were slim.

Even if their strategy provoked Saul into an angry outburst, their test was neither punitive nor unfair. The very use of the test suggests that Saul could have exercised his will to choose a more appropriate course. He was not a pawn in the hands of an evil spirit or even a victim of his own rebellion.

What did David and Jonathan's test reveal? How would someone consumed with pathological hatred behave? Perfectly normal—as it turned out, at least for short periods of time. No one observing him the first night would have guessed anything was wrong. He was with family and friends, enjoying a royal dinner. If someone had polled the guests who knew Saul casually, few would have said he was capable of violent rage.

People can become quite adept at covering up their anger. Remember, O. J. Simpson's fellow athletes saw him as a meek and mild man before his trial. They were flabbergasted when they heard the horrifying 911 recordings of OJ screaming obscenities and shouting threats in out-of-control rage at Nicole.

What was the first clue that Saul was full of hate? On the second day of the feast, Saul casually asked Jonathan, "Oh, by the way, I noticed that neither last night (so he *was* paying attention!) nor tonight," and then Saul's facade began to crack, for he couldn't bring himself to say David's name, "the *son of Jesse* hasn't been here. Why?" Everybody called him David. Saul had always called David by his name, but the king's rage was so great that he could not bring himself to say it. The next time you are in deep conflict with someone who starts calling you by another name, watch out.

After Jonathan gave his rehearsed reply, it all hit the fan. Saul's madness and pathological envy enabled him to see with instant clarity that Jonathan and David had planned this charade deliberately to check his intentions! What began as a happy family dinner now turned into a scene of electrifying violence. Saul cursed Jonathan, the son he had wanted so much to succeed him as king, accusing him of abdication in siding with David. It took nothing to set Saul off when the subject was David.

Saul ranted, "I know that you have sided with the son of Jesse to your own shame." In one sense of course Saul was correct, and this was a profound humiliation to him. Wasn't it bad enough, he reasoned, that the Lord had rejected him and chosen this "son of Jesse" (he still can't say his name)? Must Jonathan side with God too?

Furthermore, why couldn't the things that mattered most to Saul matter as much to Jonathan? Hadn't Jonathan realized that with David alive neither Jonathan nor his kingdom would ever be established? But Jonathan did not care. He was about as unmoved by the kingdom that his father offered him as was Jesus when the devil tempted him in the wilderness.

There was only one remedy for Saul. "Bring him to me, for he must die!" Jonathan tried to reason with his father. Hadn't David's actions actually benefited the king? But there could be no reasonable approach to Saul because his rage was tied to sin, not reason. So in a frenzy, Saul cast his spear at his own son. The spear missed, but Saul's words did not, for Jonathan had his answer—and it was more than he wanted to know. He left the table infuriated and humiliated, though his anger was different from his father's.

THE FLIGHT TO NOB (1 SAMUEL 21)

Once Jonathan informed David of Saul's reaction, David fled in desperation and went to the shrine at Nob. There he confronted the priest Ahimelech. David insisted that he was on an urgent mission for the king, so urgent, in fact, that he and his men hadn't had time to get food or weapons. He asked Ahimelech for bread and a sword. Why David invented this story is unclear. Perhaps he was trying to protect the priest from being involved with his escape. Or perhaps David wasn't sure if he could trust Ahimelech, since the priest's brother Ahijah had become Saul's spiritual advisor when Samuel withdrew his services.

Although David's story may have seemed at first incredible, Ahimelech gave David the only bread he had in the temple—the ceremonial holy bread. Then he gave David Goliath's sword, which had been proudly displayed at the temple. The narrator also mentions one more small but highly significant detail: Doeg the Edomite, Saul's head shepherd and one of his more sinister servants, was there at the tabernacle observing.

DAVID'S ESCAPE TO JUDAH (1 SAMUEL 22)

Saul was holding court with his Benjamite tribe of advisors when he heard the news that David and his men had escaped to Judah. Saul should have been conversing with his advisors about the affairs of state, the ever-present Philistine threat, or even praising them for services rendered. But the desperately troubled Saul had only one obsession, the man he could only refer to now as "the son of Jesse." He longed for the reassurance that he still commanded the full support of his men, yet he insulted his advisors at every turn. He had no evidence of their disloyalty, yet he accused them of having "defected" to David. That was a particularly serious charge, for while David was from the tribe of Judah, Saul was a Benjamite. He was accusing these men not only of personal betrayal but also of tribal betrayal.

His speech was pathetic and embarrassing: "Listen, men of Benjamin! Will the son of Jesse give all of you fields and vineyards? Will he make all of you commanders of thousands and commanders of hundreds?" For Saul, power obviously had become the single most important value in his view of government. But this was of no value in *God's* view of government. Saul did exactly what Samuel warned him *not* to do: He became as the kings of other nations and thus contradicted God's covenantal ideal for kingship.

"Is that why you have all conspired against me? No one tells me when my son makes a covenant with the son of Jesse. None of you is concerned about me or tells me that my son has incited my servant to lie in wait for me, as he does today." Not only did Saul show no respect for his officials, but his charges had no basis in reality. Saul was beyond reason now, and his point was very clear—if you don't hate David as much as I do, then you are my enemy. Saul's mind was made up, and it would have done no good to confuse him with the facts. He didn't want reason; he wanted revenge.

SAUL'S VENGEANCE AT NOB

In light of such a tirade, what defense could the advisors give? Silence spread over the court. Then someone spoke up and told Saul what he wanted to hear. The mercenary, Doeg the Edomite, told the king that Ahimelech had given David a sword and food and even "inquired of the Lord" for him (this last fact is not mentioned in the text, although the priest later admits that it was true).

That was all Saul needed to know! Ahimelech was ordered at once. Saul asked him, "Why have you conspired against me, you and the son of Jesse, giving him bread and a sword and inquiring of God for him, so that he has rebelled against me and lies in wait for me, as he does today?" How ironic. The only one guilty of conspiracy, rebellion, and entrapment was Saul. Such is the nature of sin to invert reality, making the abuser feel abused! Ahimelech gave a spirited, truthful, and fair defense, but it was lost on Saul.

Though we have witnessed Saul's deep descent into sin, nothing could prepare us for what happened next. Saul's verdict was quick and horrifying—death to the entire house of Ahimelech. He ordered the execution of every single priest. Even if Ahimelech had been guilty, why should everyone in his family have to die? When Saul ordered the guards to "kill the priests of the Lord, because they too have sided with David," the guards refused. They knew this was a crazed man asking them to do great evil. But Doeg, an outsider and perhaps a proselyte who wished to be accepted into the communion of Israel, was only too eager to assist. Overly eager, in fact. He systemically slaughtered "eighty-five men who wore the linen ephod." Then "he also put to the sword Nob, the town of the priests, with its men and women, its children and infants, and its cattle, donkeys and sheep."

This was wholesale destruction. How ironic that Saul had refused to obey God's orders to kill all of the Amalekites, yet he showed no reluctance to allow someone to kill his very own people. Saul's unchecked hatred for one man led to the massacre of an entire village.

The story of Doeg must alert us to the potential evil consequences of third-party help when we are in conflict with someone. Often people who display an extreme urgency to be involved have their own agenda or unacknowledged needs. Doeg's agenda seemed to be to ingratiate himself to the king and thus be close to power. Saul's advisors knew the king much better than Doeg did. Their inaction and silence would have been far more effective in helping Saul face himself. As it happened, Doeg's intervention only solidified Saul all the more in his sin.

Only Ahimelech's son Abiathar escaped the massacre unnoticed. He fled to David and told him the horrible news. David characteristically took responsibility not only for Abiathar but also for the entire massacre. He remembered seeing Doeg and feeling uneasy about his presence. "That day when Doeg the Edomite was there, I knew he would be sure to tell Saul. I am responsible for the death of your father's whole family."

THE EFFECTS OF HATE

One theme that runs through both the Old and the New Testaments is that sin is a serious matter with very serious consequences. It cannot be taken lightly, for its effects are both far-reaching and long-lasting—upon our relationship to God, to ourselves, and to others. In this episode we have seen that Saul's anger and envy led to settled hatred. We need to remember that Saul didn't begin by hating David; in fact, he loved him. But once Saul became envious of David, his unchecked and unrepentant sin led to murderous hatred. Sin, in other words, is progressive in nature.

The worst thing about hatred is that it causes a person to fall away from the love of God and the love of one another. Instead of acting for the ultimate welfare of our neighbor, hate causes us to despise, loathe, be intolerant of, and wish malice upon him. We are told that we must not hate fellow Christians (1 John 4:20) or even our enemies (Matt. 5:43-44). Hating the sin but not the sinner is the standard set by Christ (Ps. 45:7; Heb. 1:9). But we must be very cautious with all feelings of hate, even when we tell ourselves that our intense feelings are truly righteous indignation. It is so easy to become self-righteous and blind to the fact that we too are sinners in radical need of God's grace.

Yet even when we do have a righteous anger against sin and a justifiable hatred of evil, that still does not give us permission to hate the person who has sinned against us. God's intention is to set us free from all sin.

THE PROBLEM WITH HIDDEN HATRED

Hate is difficult to deal with, not only because it is the result of other sins that have been allowed to grow in us over time, but because no one ever wants to admit it! We go to great lengths to cover up our hatred. But we can't be forgiven and healed of a sin that we refuse to admit.

That is why Saul's story is so helpful to us. Though he was consumed with hatred, he refused to admit it. He may have been somewhat deranged by this time, but his behavior shows how hatred operates and the measures we will take to disguise or justify it. In fact, Saul was in such denial about his own sin that he believed *he* was the one being persecuted! We need to observe the schemes he used to hide his unjustified hatred.

HATRED CRIES, "BETRAYED!"

Saul's first argument to his advisors was in the form of a question. "Did you betray me because you thought David would give you more possessions and power than I have already given you?" This was a clever though devious question, rather like asking, "So when did you finally stop beating your wife?" It was a trap designed to manipulate the advisors through guilt. Had they betrayed him? Of course not. But neither had David.

Hatred feels justified when it can hide behind the cry, "I've been betrayed!" But, in fact, the real betrayal and unfaithfulness was on *Saul's* part. He pulled the oldest trick in the book—he accused people of what *he* was guilty of and then watched them dance like oil on a griddle because they had been manipulated into feeling guilty.

Saul's innuendo that others were responsible for his well-being since he had been so good to them was exactly wrong. He had not been good to them; he had failed them miserably as a leader. As king, he was responsible for *their* well-being. Saul's attempt to make them feel guilty for supposed disloyalty was based on an utterly false notion of loyalty. Saul did not encourage his advisors to consider the facts and come to their own conclusion. For Saul, loyalty meant that his associates should hate David as much as he did. Any deviation from this point of view was considered betrayal. But if loyalty is to have any meaning, it must be based upon truth and not on a diseased view of reality.

HATRED PLAYS THE VICTIM

Hatred is aggressive, but it often plays the victim. Saul insisted that he was being persecuted, attacked, and victimized. What an inversion of truth! He was the abuser, the persecutor who relentlessly pursued David. Saul claimed David was maligning him, when it was Saul who slandered David. Saul acted as if he were the only one in anguish, yet there was not an ounce of concern for all the pain he had inflicted upon David, not to mention on his own son Jonathan and his daughter Michal. His total self-centeredness was exceeded only by his paranoid deception.

Why is playing the victim so important for maintaining our hate? Because it lets us off the hook. It's another way of insisting on our innocence. It enables us to indulge in self-pity, which further justifies our hate. Saul reasoned like this: "I really don't like doing this to David. I feel badly about being so angry. But I was just innocently being a king, and the next thing I knew, David tried to take my kingdom away from me! I am only protecting my rights." The text of 1 Samuel shows that this was self-justification at its worst.

Hatred is by nature an aggressive force, but it likes to appear weak and dependent. How could such an aggressive energy possibly work out its intentions while masquerading behind weakness? For Saul it really was quite simple. He let someone else do his dirty work while he hid behind the victim mask. Doeg acted out all of Saul's rage against David without Saul having to soil his own hands. Yet as is often the case when aggression is hidden, once the "victim" approach failed to work, as with Jonathan, the pretense was finally dropped. The mask came off, and Saul's hatred stood out with instant and terrifying clarity.

HATRED MUST FIND AN EXCUSE

Very few of us want to admit to something as heinous as hatred because it impugns our view of ourselves. That explains why Saul was so obsessed with his need to vilify David. He had to justify his own hateful behavior. It is the nature of evil (hate in this case) to conceal and disguise itself. So perhaps it is not surprising that hateful people often tend to gravitate toward piety for the disguise and concealment it can offer them.

That is why there is a remarkably visible element of self-righteousness in those who hate. If they can label another as bad, it allows them to feel justified in hating. With their self-righteousness intact, they can unleash their hatred and turn a blind eye to the fact that there seems to be no correlation between the provocation and their response. Such evil is rarely committed by people who feel uncertain about their righteousness or who question their own motives. As Scott Peck has said in his book *People of the Lie:* "The evil in this world is committed by these . . . Pharisees of our own day, the self-righteous. . . . It is out of their failure to put themselves on trial that their evil arises."

The truth is, the victims of our hatred are often nothing but scapegoats. But haters need scapegoats in order to feel virtuous and self-righteous. Saul modeled the same scapegoating characteristic that all haters share in common—the necessity to relieve the tension by fixing the blame on someone else. They project their own evil onto the world. They never see themselves as evil; they consequently see much evil in others. This is why hateful people are so destructive. They believe they are attempting to destroy evil "out there." But as Peck says, "The problem is that they misplace the locus of the evil. Instead of destroying others, they should be destroying the sickness in themselves."

HATRED MUST DEFACE THE ENEMY

Hatred always diminishes its object's essence so that he or she no longer has a unique identity or even a name, but rather is considered only a thing or a possession. Saul demonstrated this by refusing to refer to David by name. Holocaust survivor and Nobel prizewinner Elie

Wiesel has described this phenomenon under the Nazis: "The person who was first a person became a prisoner and the prisoner became a number and the number became an ash." That is the inevitable path of hatred, as the ashes of Nob and the German prison camps remind us.

Hatred reduces a person to "the one who did that awful thing to me." The hated have no identity outside of their perceived injury to the hater. In reality, of course, that isn't true. There is vastly more to a person than his or her sin, whether real or imagined. But not to the one doing the hating. I remember feeling deeply offended and hurt by what I considered a betrayal on the part of an old friend. I knew I needed to forgive her, but the wound just would not close.

Then I remembered when we first met and the help she had been to me in my younger years. Suddenly I was able to see her for who she was apart from the deep pain she caused me. This friend was so much more than a disloyal person. Although I was not struggling at that point with hate, still I had to repent for reducing her to less than what she truly was.

Saul revealed what happens when we refuse to repent of blind hatred. To dehumanize another through one's hatred is to dehumanize oneself. Saul's very hatred began to make him more of a caricature and less of a man. Eventually, all we can see in Saul is the raw power that he used only to destroy others and himself.

HATRED THAT IS DEMONIC

What was it that really goaded Saul? Seemingly, it was the very things that made David so appealing. Saul hated the way people responded to David's warmheartedness, his way with people, his ability to win the hearts of Saul's own children.

Then something happened that is terrifying to ponder. At first Saul's sins seemed to be of the "flesh-and-blood" variety. He was envious and hateful, judgmental and proud, outraged and obsessed with David. That, of course, is bad enough. But over time Saul's sins hardened, and his refusal to repent deepened. Saul unwittingly made himself vulnerable to an even deeper evil: demonic oppression. Through his persistent and unrelenting sin, a demonic "evil spirit" was allowed access into

Saul's inner being. No longer are we merely dealing with a man who must confess sin in order to be healed. We are now dealing with a demonically oppressed man who needs deliverance from evil as well.

Think about it. When did Saul's rage become the most virulent and out of control? When David exercised the divine gifts he had received to accomplish God's purposes. When David played the harp, Saul threw his spear at him. When David succeeded in battle, Saul plotted to kill him.

It was when God's Spirit was the most visible in David that we see the evil spirit most visibly operating through Saul. The demons hate it when believers exercise their spiritual gifts, because God's people use these capabilities to build God's kingdom on earth. The enemy tries desperately to block God's ministry and work. In this conflict, David was warring not only against the sins of "flesh and blood," but against an even deeper evil power from another realm. This battle was spiritual in nature, for it represented not merely a human conflict but the clash of spiritual kingdoms.

Clearly, the evil spirit in Saul was intent on destroying David. But that does not let Saul off the hook. This spirit had gained access to Saul through the king's rebellion and sin. He had cooperated with the power of evil.

Hatred then, whether demonic or human, is evil and destructive. Hate blinds us and causes us to see monsters where humans exist. Ironically, though hate's intent is to murder, whether physically or through character assassination, hatred can also energize and give life to its carrier. Saul's rage kept him going and even gave his life meaning as he pursued David. As psychiatrist J. R. Lifton points out: "One needs that target in order to go on hating because one needs one's hatred in order to go on feeling alive." Ultimately, though, hate distorts the personality, scars the soul, and dehumanizes and destroys its carrier, as we saw with Saul.

WHAT TO DO ABOUT HATE

We know hate destroys us, but knowing that does not deliver us from its clutches. How do we get rid of hate?

Admit It

I remember a time when I recognized hate within me. A woman I knew had caused a great deal of pain to some people for whom I cared deeply. I was grieved over what she had done, but one day I had to face my feelings. I was shocked to see how deep my hate was. It was humbling to acknowledge that kind of poison within me. But having identified it, I realized that only God could really change my heart. I could no more love her sincerely than fly. What was my responsibility? I wondered.

As I reflected on what I had learned from having walked with God, I knew instantly that the first thing I had to do was stop gossiping. Whenever the people she had wounded and I got together, we would discuss all of the things she had done. It felt like such a little thing in light of what this person had done. Yet where did gossiping lead me? To joy and freedom? Hardly. It simply caused me to spiral into the pit of bitterness and revenge-seeking. I clearly saw that although I could not make my heart loving toward this person, I could stop talking about her in a negative way. So I did. It is almost embarrassing to admit how much it helped. For one thing, I was not continually dredging up all of that pain.

Refuse Evil

Then a new challenge emerged. I would be going along fine when suddenly a thought about that person would come. All of the old poison would rise up in me. I told God that I needed fresh help for this new problem. The next day I read a verse in the Bible from Paul's letter to Corinth: "Let every thought be held in captivity to Christ Jesus." As I pondered the meaning of that in light of my problem, a new idea came to me. It sounds painfully obvious, but it had not occurred to me that it was my choice whether or not to feed on hateful thoughts. Each time the fiery dart was launched in my mind, I had always followed it into the pit of bitterness, retracing the painful steps all over again. I prayed that I would become aware of the first intrusion of a negative thought. It would be far easier to avoid the journey of hatred altogether, rather than give in to the thought for a while and then try to reverse my steps.

That same day I was listening to the radio and heard a psychologist discuss what she called "stop thoughts." Her point was that if we do not want to entertain destructive thoughts, we have that option. She suggested that after refusing them entry into our minds, we should get up and immediately do something active.

Pray for Obedience

It was then that I realized that I had not distinguished between temptation and sin. I was being tempted to the sin of hatred by these thoughts, but I did not have to succumb. So when the thoughts popped into my mind, I turned to the Lord and said, "I do not want to hate, but I cannot love. Please give me the strength not to indulge in these thoughts, for they only make me miserable and separated from you. From now on, with your help, I am choosing not to allow them into my heart." God did help me, yet it was clear how important my own obedience was. I took several other steps in the process and only in retrospect did I see that each tiny step was preparing me for the biggest step of all—to pray for the woman who had caused all the pain.

Choose Love

One day God seemed to say to me, "Becky, you have never prayed for her. Why don't you?"

"No way," I said to God, "because if I do, you might make me like her." And that was the last thing I wanted to happen. My fear was that what God meant by "love your enemy" was to pretend that what she had done really didn't matter. I feared that to love meant I had to lie to myself, saying that no injustice had been done. But the next day I read in my devotions, "Love your enemy," and it dawned on me for the first time that Jesus wasn't saying, "If you love her, she'll quit being your enemy." No, Jesus acknowledged that we will have enemies, people who can be dangerous and are untrustworthy. We can recognize them as enemies, but we are still called to love them. I wasn't being asked to lie to myself; I was being asked to choose love.

John Calvin was right. Grace really is irresistible. I gave in and prayed for her the next day. The moment I said her name, I started to cry. My hard heart was no match for God's love. God wasn't asking me to pretend that what she had done wasn't wrong. But prayer connects us to the very being of God and his love. Therefore, I found myself asking the kinds of questions I couldn't ask before because hate had filled a part of my soul: What is her story? What kind of background did she come from? What shaped her that she could do such a thing to someone? And then I prayed for myself. What blinders was I wearing that prevented my seeing *any* good in her?

Slowly, in this way my heart began to soften. I can't remember when it was precisely, but one day I realized that the poison was gone. She did not become an intimate friend. Jesus did not promise that loving an enemy would suddenly turn that person into a trustworthy friend. But I can honestly say that as I obeyed what God showed me, he changed my heart of stone to a heart of flesh.

Several years after hearing Corrie ten Boom tell her story to that audience in Portland, Oregon, I was visiting Ethel Renwick, the woman who led me to Christ. Her husband Frank had died, and I was there for the funeral. Unexpectedly, she received a telephone call from Corrie, who was speaking in the area. They had been close friends, and Corrie asked Ethel and her children to come to the home where she was staying. Ethel invited me to go along. It was the privilege of a lifetime to sit in a cozy living room and listen and watch this woman. I don't think I have ever met a person who so radiated the love of Christ. There was a spiritual power in her presence that truly came from above.

I told her how moved I had been when I had heard her speak years before, especially when she told her story about the prison guard. She said, "You know, someone might hear that story and think God was an ogre to demand such obedience. I had dragged my feet all the way to Germany because I didn't want to go. I gave a talk on forgiveness only to discover the one man that I hadn't been able to forgive sitting right in front of me on the very first night! But now I realize that the call to go to Germany, along with the guard being there, was God-ordered so that *I* could be set free! I was resisting my own healing! God does not require obedience because he is mean, but because he loves us and he does not want us to carry within our souls the things that will destroy us."

Corrie had said in her lecture that Jesus' command to love our enemies is, at one level, impossible. Yet with God nothing is impossible. What God requires is obedience, both in our behavior and in our prayers that cry out to him for help. Then God will help us to do what we must do but could never do on our own.

Maybe you are reading this, and you believe that there is no way you will ever be able to conquer your deep resentment and hostility toward someone. But Corrie ten Boom reminds us that with God all things are possible. He needs our cooperation, but the goal is for our own freedom and healing! We must not allow God's power and love to be blocked by our sin. We must not allow sin in, or else it will grow and take on a life of its own.

My deliverance from hate did not happen in a moment as it did with Corrie ten Boom. It was a process in which I was involved every step of the way. But the result was the same: I was free!

QUESTIONS AND REFLECTIONS

1. Have you ever had to overcome hate? What was the hardest part in letting it go? What enabled you to conquer it?

2. In this chapter what disguises did you see used to cover hate? (Playing the victim, claiming betrayal, etc.) Can you think of others?

3. Of the steps suggested for overcoming hate, which is the hardest for you? Why?

4. What tends to drive your hatred (envy, greed, lust, etc.)? Why?

Chapter Six

Love:
The Remedy for Hate

Have you ever noticed that the one thing virtually everyone agrees upon is love? What unites skeptic and believer, people on the opposite side of nearly any position, is that "love makes the world go 'round." Most people pay lip service to love. It's in our songs; it's on our televisions, in our films and our literature. Despite all the things that divide us as a nation, most still believe that love transcends our problems.

In one of his books, Martin Luther King, Jr., said he believed that love could give us the courage to face the uncertainties of our future as a nation in the area of race relations. He declared that "love is the only force capable of transforming an enemy into a friend. We never get rid of an enemy by meeting hate with hate; we get rid of an enemy by getting rid of enmity. By its very nature, hate destroys and tears down; by its very nature, love creates and builds up. Love transforms with redemptive power." *(Strength to Love)*

How marvelous, we say. Love is the answer! But we must ask, What is love? What does it actually mean to truly love in the midst of the ambiguities and complexities of life? For example, suppose you have been hated and maligned by an enemy. An enemy's hatred is a powerful force. So powerful, in fact, that whenever we feel we are the object of someone's hate, the temptation is to hate back. But Jesus commanded us to love our enemies instead and even to pray for those who persecute us.

Even more difficult, what if our conflict is with a cherished friend or family member? Is it possible to keep a cherished relationship from turning into one of enmity? Consider the conflicts that faced Jonathan.

Jonathan loved his father, but he saw his father's sin. He wanted to be loyal as a son, but he was horrified by his father's actions. What did love demand of Jonathan when his loyalty to his father collided with his loyalty to David? How was Jonathan supposed to follow the biblical injunction to honor one's father, when Saul was asking him to destroy someone? What was Jonathan to do when the only way to love his neighbor as himself necessitated breaking away from his father? Jonathan was a son *and* a friend. He sought to be loving and loyal in both relationships, but it proved for him to be an agonizing and impossible dilemma.

The story of Jonathan and David is often used as an example of the highest expression of true friendship. But their association was more than a celebration of friendship alone. Jonathan reveals the deeper issues involved in caring about someone—the wrenching conflicts, profound tensions, and costly loyalty that practicing true love requires. David and Jonathan's covenant loyalty for each other offers guidelines that will help us as we struggle to learn how to love wisely and well in difficult situations.

LOVE SEEKS THE TRUTH

When people think of the word *love,* they often think of a relationship without tension or conflict. In one sense, that was true of the early stages of Jonathan and David's friendship. When Jonathan first met David, after the battle with Goliath, he was deeply impressed. David had spoken to Saul about his faith in the Lord, perhaps at some length, and Jonathan felt instantly drawn to this courageous young man. David, for his part, felt the same way. Jonathan made a covenant with David because they were one in spirit and because "he loved him as himself." (1 Sam. 18:1-4)

But it wasn't long until their covenant was severely tested. When

David came to Jonathan in distress, convinced that Saul was trying to kill him, Jonathan's loyalty was put on the line. Would he be true to his friend or to his father? What standards would Jonathan use to determine to whom he should be loyal? After all, the Bible says to "honor your father and your mother, so that you may live long." But the Bible also commands, "Love your neighbor as yourself." Many Christians consider this a New Testament view. But when Jesus called for this kind of love, he was in line with the true Old Testament teaching (Lev. 19:17, 18b, 34). Was it reasonable or even possible for Jonathan to obey both of these commands?

We tend to think that Jonathan's love for and loyalty to David was so profound that he supported his friend without blinking an eye. But there was more than deep emotional sentiment in Jonathan's decision to be loyal to David. Jonathan was committed to seeking the truth.

When David told Jonathan that Saul was determined to kill him, Jonathan did not want to believe it. "Never! You are not going to die! Look, my father doesn't do anything, great or small, without confiding in me. Why would he hide this from me? It's not so!" (1 Sam. 20:2) But Jonathan listened carefully to David's argument that Saul would never tell his son of his murderous intent, because Saul knew of their friendship. Jonathan didn't try to defend his father; he knew David was innocent.

How did Jonathan know what to do? He submitted his profound friendship and love for David, and his sense of duty to his father, to the standard of objective truth. That was why he was willing to help David put Saul to the test at the royal dinner during the festival of the New Moon. He needed to test David's fears as well as his father's heart. A lesser man might have either immediately accepted David's conclusion or blindly defended his father out of misguided loyalty. But Jonathan did not allow his emotions to be the interpreter of reality. Instead, he showed us that we cannot love a person wisely or well if we are not committed to seeking the truth.

Truth matters when it concerns love, even when it involves painful disclosures about a loved one. How often have we heard parents of children on drugs say that it was only when they finally rejected all the false assurances and faced the ugly truth about their child that they were truly in a position to help?

The task before Jonathan, to see his father objectively in the light of truth, is one of the most painful, difficult things an adult child is required to do. To seek the truth may involve overcoming feelings of disloyalty. It may mean letting go of one's need to protect or cover for a loved one. It may produce deep feelings of insecurity. It is hard, but it is necessary if one is to love wisely and well.

Sometimes love requires more than seeking truth. It involves *speaking* the truth as well, which is often even more difficult.

LOVE SPEAKS THE TRUTH

Once Jonathan understood the situation clearly, he did not passively sit back and do nothing. He loved his father enough to tell him the truth. When on a previous occasion Saul informed his son that he planned to kill David, Jonathan not only tried to persuade his father not to do this; he told him he was wrong. His sister Michal deceived her father outright, but Jonathan did not. He had the courage to speak the truth and say, in essence, "Dad, David hasn't hurt you. Put away your anger." And at the New Moon Festival dinner, Jonathan again dared to ask, "Why should he be put to death? What has he done?"

Saul was wrong, and without showing disrespect, Jonathan told him so. It wasn't up to Jonathan to convince Saul, but he did feel an obligation to at least help him face the truth. The covenant relationship of love always demands that we try to see the truth and, if led by God, often to speak it, even if it is painful. We do this because love is as committed to people's character as it is to their comfort.

A therapist friend of mine, whom I will call Ann, began seeing a client I will call Mary. Mary was a severe kleptomaniac. She had consulted countless therapists over the years, but what made Ann seem a bit different in Mary's eyes was that this therapist was "religious." Although the counseling seemed to be going well, Ann felt things were still on a superficial level. One day she did something rather unorthodox. She asked Mary, "Do you believe in God?"

"Oh, I'm not very religious," Mary replied, "but I know that I'm really a good person. And if there's a God, I will be okay."

Ann was incredulous. "Wait a minute, Mary. You have been in my office telling me how desperate you are to overcome your addiction to stealing, and how ashamed you feel to have been arrested so many times. You have told me how horrified you are that you can't even shop in most of the downtown stores because of your record. Do you truly believe it when you say you are a good person?"

Mary looked stunned and sat quietly. Then she asked, "Tell me the truth. I mean, I know I'm a klepto, but do you think I have a *deeper* problem than that? Do you think that I'm *not* okay?"

Ann paused for a moment, then took a deep breath, and said, "No, I don't think you're okay. And do you know *why* I know you're not? Because I know that *I'm* not either, and that no one else is. Mary, one of the reasons I am a Christian is because Jesus refuses to lie to me. He tells me I'm in trouble. I may not struggle with the same symptoms as you do, but we all have the same underlying problem of sin. And our sins drove Christ to his death to make amends for us, and to make us right before God. Scripture tells us that if we stop playing games and admit the truth, Jesus can help us become who we're meant to be."

"So what you are telling me," Mary asked, "is that you're not okay, and I'm not okay, but that's all right because Jesus came to help people like us?" It was moving to hear Ann describe the profound discovery that dawned in Mary's mind. She didn't have to hide from the deeper truth anymore.

"You know what?" Mary asked. "I always *knew* I wasn't okay! But nobody ever had the guts to tell me that before. My other therapists told me I had to build up my self-esteem, that my problem was that I didn't accept my lovability. And in one way they were absolutely right. But the problem was, I couldn't build a loving view of myself without facing my mess. Every time they told me how wonderful I was, it just made me more insecure, because I knew that there was still something terribly wrong with me. You are the first person to ever tell me my problem is sin and that *that* problem is deeper than my symptoms. Isn't it funny that I knew it all along? I just needed someone to help me face it." That experience was the beginning of Mary's conversion to Christ.

No doubt many of the therapists working with Mary were committed to helping her. But what they failed to do was tell her the truth, maybe because they did not understand it themselves. Mary is an excellent example of what Jesus meant when he said that "you will know the truth, and the truth will set you free." While hearing the truth does not necessarily mean receiving and accepting it, as was the case with Saul, still love, if it is to have any meaning at all, must first and foremost be committed to seeking and speaking the truth.

When to speak painful truth and when to remain silent and pray is a difficult and complex issue. In my experience I've often felt that those who are terribly eager to speak should not, and those who are fearful and reluctant perhaps should. Ultimately, it must be a Spirit-led decision.

"Oh, but even if I spoke the truth, it would not make any difference," we may say. Think how easy it would have been for Jonathan to rationalize: "Why bother telling Dad the truth. He always has to be right. He never listens to correction. It won't make the slightest difference." But how a person responds to the truth is not the point. What Saul chose to do with the truth was *Saul's* responsibility, not Jonathan's. Jonathan's task was to speak the truth with love and with respect. And he did.

LOVE GRIEVES FOR THE RIGHT REASONS

Though Saul demonstrated very little regard for Jonathan's life—he tried to kill him twice—Jonathan didn't experience much grief at his father's treatment of him. Ironically, the first time was immediately after an amazing military coup in which Jonathan had put his own life on the line for his father and his country and single-handedly defeated the Philistines. Saul made the soldiers vow that they would not eat until they had defeated their enemy. His decision was a disastrous one, of course, for it made the men weak and thus unable to fight. Jonathan ate honey, not knowing about the vow. Upon discovering this, the king decided to kill his son, fearful that Yahweh might be angry a vow had been broken. Saul relented, but only after the entire army demanded that Jonathan's life be spared. Jonathan's father was willing to end his son's life in order to protect his job.

Saul's next attempt to kill his son was at the royal dinner during the New Moon Festival. When Jonathan gave the king David's excuse for not being present at the festivities, Saul cursed Jonathan and then threw his spear at him. Saul's clear intent was to kill him. Jonathan did not speak, but left the table.

It would have been easy for Jonathan to interpret Saul's behavior toward him as profound personal rejection. If Jonathan had been alive today, he no doubt would have scheduled an appointment with his therapist. One could imagine the therapist asking, "So tell me, Jonathan, when did you begin to experience these rejection issues related to your father?"

"Oh, well, maybe it was when I felt his spear whistling by my head," Jonathan might have answered. "Do you think I'm overreacting to make an appointment with you every time my dad tries to kill me?"

But the remarkable thing is that Jonathan never seemed to interpret Saul's behavior as personal rejection. Yet *Saul* took virtually everything as personal rejection, so why didn't Jonathan? When Jonathan left the table in such fierce anger and deep grief, was it because of his father's despicable treatment of him? No. Jonathan left, we are told, because "he was grieved at his father's shameful treatment *of David."*

Now wait a moment, we say. How could any man be that selfless? Was Jonathan simply in denial and refusing to do his own "grief work"? But he *did* grieve, as the text tells us. However, he grieved over the *true* source of his father's problem.

"May the Lord be with you *as he has been* with my father," Jonathan said to David. Jonathan knew that God's Spirit had departed from Saul. He saw that the real issue was not his father's rejection of him, or even of David, but God's rejection of his father because of Saul's rebellion.

That was what Jonathan grieved about. That was why he didn't get stuck emotionally in wondering if Saul's behavior was aimed at him personally. His father was in rebellion against God, and the proof was the grievous way Saul treated David. It made Jonathan sad and furious. But by accurately diagnosing his father's problem, Jonathan saved himself a great deal of pain.

I meet many adults who struggle with issues related to one or both of their parents. But very few of them ever ask the key question, What kind of relationship does my mother or father have with God? One wonders how much grief could be spared if wounded children would evaluate their parents in light of where they are with God rather than solely on how they were treated by them. This does not mean that godly parents won't make horrendous mistakes with their children, or that our pain will hurt any less because a parent was out of sync with God when they raised us. But if a parent has been in spiritual rebellion, as was Saul, one can expect that he or she will evidence many other significant problems as well.

Jonathan was not what was wrong with Saul. *David* was not what was wrong either. What was wrong with Saul was that he was at war with the Creator of the universe. Even so, Jonathan "took the bullets," as most children of rebellious parents do. Yet he did so without fighting back, and without giving in to the hatred his father was venting.

LOVE KNOWS ITS PRIORITIES

What if Jonathan had interpreted Saul's rage as personal rejection, and was willing to do whatever it took to gain his father's approval? What if he felt that he was responsible for making his father happy, no matter what was asked? It is terrifying to consider the consequences, for the only way Jonathan would have pleased Saul was to kill his best friend.

When we want to show love to someone we care about, we should ask ourselves what kind of fruit will be produced by pleasing the person and keeping the peace. Will this honor God? Is what the person is asking actually the best thing for them? Is it best for others in that person's life? If pleasing someone is destructive for anyone involved, then pleasing them is not the loving thing to do.

It certainly was not in Saul's best interest for Jonathan to have "loved" him the way he wanted to be loved. It was the truth that set Jonathan free. By evaluating Saul's demands in the light of genuine love, Jonathan prevented serious harm to his friend—and ultimately kept Saul from having David's blood on his hands.

What if a well-meaning believer had approached Jonathan and said, "Well, you sure aren't honoring your father like the Bible says you should!" Would that assessment have been accurate? Not at all, for Jonathan *did* honor his father; he told Saul the truth. Furthermore, when he realized his father was in deep rebellion against God, Jonathan refused to assist him in his destructive efforts by telling him what he wanted to hear, as Doeg did. In that, Jonathan revealed the tough, painful side of love. Love is not manipulated by guilt or fear. It is not so willing to find acceptance that it fails to see the reality of the situation.

LOVE GETS ANGRY WITHOUT HARMING OTHERS

Many Christians think it is wrong to experience anger. But anger isn't always a case of sin. Sometimes our anger is justified, and we need to give ourselves permission to experience painful feelings.

Perhaps we should learn from Jonathan. He demonstrated that you can be angry and still be loving. After what happened at the New Moon Festival dinner, Jonathan was outraged, and it was written all over his face. He felt such emotional turmoil that he couldn't eat. The vital difference, however, between his anger and Saul's was that Saul lashed out at anyone who crossed him. Jonathan, on the other hand, contained his anger at Saul so that it harmed no one. His motive wasn't self-indulgence or self-pity, but righteous indignation. It was just *wrong* for Saul to treat David so unjustly! Even so, that did not mean Jonathan could act out his rage as he pleased, for even hate of hatred is dangerous.

Simply put, the end did not justify the means in Jonathan's time any more than it does in ours. Yet, how often have we seen Christians, believing they are on the side of righteousness, smugly use underhanded or mean-spirited ways to attack their enemies? Jonathan's anger against Saul was justified, but he didn't respond disrespectfully to his father. Instead, he left the scene before his anger caused him do something he regretted. Even when our anger is "righteous," we must always treat people with respect.

LOVE IS COSTLY

For both Jonathan and David, the stakes of friendship were very high. David needed Jonathan's loyalty for immediate protection, but Jonathan also asked David to be loyal. "But show me unfailing kindness like that of the Lord as long as I live, so that I may not be killed, and do not ever cut off your kindness from my family—not even when the Lord has cut off every one of David's enemies from the face of the earth." (1 Sam. 20: 14-15)

This was a remarkable speech because *David* was the one in danger, not Jonathan. But he knew that the future of the throne rested with David, and that David's worst enemy was Jonathan's own father. When Jonathan delivered the sad message of Saul's reaction to David, he reassured his friend again that they were bound together in sworn friendship. "The Lord is witness between you and me, and between your descendants and my descendants forever." They wept together, but David wept the most.

It was an awesome moment, clearly revealing how costly their bond of loyalty was. For David, fleeing to safety would mean losing contact with the best friend he ever had. He would never again meet the equal of Jonathan. It must have been horribly painful. In David's later years, we can't help but wonder if as king he might have avoided some of his heartbreaking problems if Jonathan had been there to speak the truth to him and offer his wise counsel.

But Jonathan paid a higher price. He knew that the tide had turned. His own succession to kingship was less and less in question. His father had failed as Israel's monarch, and because Saul's rebellion was against God's choice in David, it meant danger for his father's life as well as his own. In the ancient world, new rulers were never merciful to those who claimed any right to the throne. But David promised loyalty not only to Jonathan but to his heirs, and he proved to be a man of his word.

When Jonathan addressed David by saying, "May the Lord be with you as he has been with my father," this was a stunning endorsement of his friend and an equally stunning rejection of his own family's continuing dynasty. From a contemporary vantage point, this doesn't seem like such a big deal, for David was obviously a heroic and destined figure. But Jonathan said this while his own father was still in power as sovereign king of the nation. David at this point had no overt power, no military might, no title. It is remarkable that Jonathan had such discernment.

Throughout history God's people have been willing to pay the price for truth and loyalty. A gray-haired woman of sixty with a heavy German accent spoke to a congregation in Tennessee. She was a Jew who had been captured as a teenager and sent to prison camp during the second world war. Her story was not unlike other stories of the tragic suffering of prisoners inside German concentration camps.

After months of abuse and malnutrition that led to starvation, she realized that if she had any hope of escaping she had to do it while she still had some strength. Having just graduated from high school, she saw women just a few years older than her who already looked elderly. She plotted an escape carefully, and tried to leave no detail to chance.

On the night of her escape she had maneuvered every challenge successfully. There was only one hurdle left—a literal one. She had to scale a barbed wire fence to get outside the compound. She was halfway up the fence when the S.S. guard on duty spotted her. He screamed for her to stop, and at gunpoint demanded that she drop down. She did, her knees and legs badly bleeding. She began sobbing, realizing that her only hope of escape had just vanished.

But to her astonishment she heard the guard say, "Ellie? Is that you? It can't be possible!" She looked into his face and realized it was Rolf, a fellow classmate who had been her best friend in middle school. They had shared so many secret dreams and aspirations then. But now it was wartime, and they were on opposite sides. "Oh, Rolf, go ahead and kill me. Please! I have no reason to live. I have lost all hope. Get it over with and let me die now. There's nothing to live for anyway."

"Ellie, you are so wrong. There is everything to live for so long as you know *who* to live for. I'm going to let you go. I'll guard you until you climb the wall and get on the other side. But would you promise me one thing?"

Ellie looked at him incredulously, thinking he must be joking, but she could see his intensity and knew he meant every word. "What is it, Rolf?" she asked.

"Promise me when you get on the other side and become free, that you will ask one question continuously until someone answers it for you. Ask, 'Why does Jesus Christ make life worth living?' Promise me, Ellie! He's the only reason to live. Promise me you'll ask until you get the answer."

"Yes, I promise, I promise!" she shouted. As she furiously climbed the fence she felt guilty. *I would have said anything,* she thought to herself, *to get out of this hellhole.*

As she dropped to the other side into freedom, she heard several deafening shots. She turned to look as she ran, convinced that Rolf had changed his mind and amazed that his bullets had missed. To her horror, she saw that other S.S. guards, having realized that Rolf allowed and aided her escape, had killed him on the spot. It was as she ran to her freedom that it dawned on her that Rolf died for her that she might know this Jesus. She wondered who this Jesus Christ was, that someone would lay down his own life so that she could know him.

"And so, I did exactly as Rolf told me to do. I kept asking and asking, until one day I met someone who answered his question. I am a Christian today because Rolf sacrificed his life for me."

What God requires of his followers has not changed. Rolf and Jonathan paid a great price for their loyalty. The cost of love has always been high.

THE LOVE OF GOD FOR US

Seeing love demonstrated by another is a powerful experience. But what ultimately sets us free to love is when we consider God's extravagant love for us in spite of our shortcomings and moral flaws. What melts our hearts is when we reflect on how time after time God has forgiven us and been tender and patient with us, until we finally learned what he was trying to teach us.

How can we harbor malice towards another when the *only* One who is altogether perfect continues to love us despite our sin? That God could be holy and just, yet also merciful and loving, is nearly beyond our comprehension. Yet when we think of it, the conflict between justice and mercy occurs again and again in real life.

In my book *Hope Has Its Reasons* I told the story of how once in a courtroom I witnessed a person being sentenced for a crime. On the one hand, the principle of absolute justice seemed to reign supreme. It was bone-chilling to see the impersonal nature of the law. Justice did not care if the individual being tried was someone's son, sibling, or friend. It was irrelevant whether the person was deeply sorry and would never do it again, or if he was carrying emotional baggage of his own. He had committed a crime. He had to pay.

But another perspective was present in that courtroom—the law of love. Just as the judge was giving the sentence, a middle-aged man suddenly broke into racking sobs. He was clearly the father of the person on trial, and his anguish changed everything. For a split second we all saw the accused through a different lens. This was not a defendant who had committed a crime. This was somebody's child grown up, a child still adored and treasured by his father. Even the judge paused, but he had his job to do and he resumed sentencing. Later, as everyone filed out, I heard the father say, "I have never felt so helpless in my entire life. If only I could have done something. I would have gladly paid the price if I could." That was the first time I had ever been in a courtroom. But the overwhelming memory that I carry with me was not the trial itself but the response of the parent wishing he could have taken the place of his child.

The judge's job is to sentence. The parent's heart is to stand in for the child. Stand in for the child? There is our clue. When love comes face to face with crisis and suffering in the one who is loved, its first impulse is to stand in, to substitute. Don't we sometimes wish we could bear the suffering of loved ones if it would spare them the trauma? I have never met parents who did not say of their critically ill child, "How I wish it could have been me instead."

That is exactly what God felt. *And that is exactly what God did.* He took our place. When the judgment had to fall, it fell on Christ, our substitute. Here is the remarkable fact: We are the proud sinners, but the final—and willing—victim of our sin and pride is God. The concept of substitution, or standing in, lies at the heart of the highest love of all and therefore at the heart of our salvation. To not allow God's love to permeate our hearts, to refuse to let go of our hatred for our enemies, means we have never really believed one incontestable fact: Christ died for us while we were yet sinners.

QUESTIONS AND REFLECTIONS

1. What has Jonathan taught you about honoring your parents?

2. When has love required you to speak painful truth? Was the outcome positive or negative? What did you learn from the experience?

3. Where have you seen love that is costly? How has it affected you?

4. What does the Cross teach us about how to love?

5. What are some of the complexities we must face in learning how to love wisely and well?

Chapter Seven

Rebellion:
When the Heart Turns Hard

I have a friend who learned his cholesterol count was extremely high, and his doctor told him he needed to lose some weight. He went to a registered dietician, expecting to hear from her the regular pitch: watch your calories, avoid high-fat foods, start exercising, and so on. Instead, she began, "There are basic laws of the universe that you have been violating. There is an objective basis to reality, and taking care of your health is part of that reality. Either you accept and conform to the way your body functions best, or you can continue to break the laws and suffer the inevitable consequences as you are now. Your high cholesterol count is a blessing in disguise, because it's telling you that you have gone off course."

She continued, "In order to change, you first must be very honest with yourself. You have not abided by the laws of nature, or you wouldn't be here with this cholesterol count. Then you need to change your way of thinking and get your mind in alignment with reality. Next you must get your will in alignment with the truth, too. Once you get your thinking and your will straight, then we'll talk about proper food and exercise. But unless you are willing to admit that you have been wrong and are committed to making the changes, I can't help you. It's your choice."

As I listened to him tell the story, I was fascinated by her description of the intrinsic structure of reality. As Christians, we know that reality is not subjective. The universe has a moral configuration, because we are a created planet and a created people, formed by a moral and loving God. The key to living a meaningful life is to be in a vital relationship with our Creator, and with his help to align ourselves with his will and conform to his moral structure. Whether we believe in the true God or not, when we violate the God-given principles of this universe, we will go awry, because God's ways simply do not fluctuate. His principles continue to operate whether we adhere to them or not. It's the old adage that you can't break the laws that govern life; you can only break yourself when you refuse to follow them.

The dietician's approach also surprised my friend because he realized that what she was really asking him to do was to repent. By asking him to change the way he perceived reality and to conform his behavior to the way things truly are, she *was* calling for one kind of "repentance." As John White says in his illuminating book *Changing on the Inside,* " . . . Repentance is in essence a shift in point of view, a facing of and response to reality." As Christians, we know that God is the central reality of this universe. Thus the essence of positive and lasting change always involves aligning oneself with this reality. We face reality—about ourselves, about our environment, and hopefully about God himself—when we submit to God's truth. The deepest repentance of all is spiritual in nature—going back to God and establishing a relationship with him. Whether it's the first time or the fiftieth, real, profound, and positive change of character calls for a returning to God and a following of his ways. My friend concluded, "It never dawned on me that repentance takes place in so many realms. Because I knew I wasn't committing any major *moral* sin, it didn't occur to me that I could be violating God's physical laws, which also have serious consequences."

My friend was willing to change to improve his health and, hopefully, his quality of life. But how do we explain those who refuse to bend—those who, no matter how bad it gets, still stubbornly refuse to admit to their problems? Putting it another way, how much does a person have to lose before he or she is willing to repent?

Those are some of the questions that Saul's life forces us to ask, questions he never asked himself. Nothing worked for him, yet still he persisted. The more his attempts to destroy David were foiled, the more he tried from other angles. Why didn't Saul ever ask himself, "What am I doing wrong?" Why did he never question his own map of reality and submit it to God for realignment?

Saul is in fact the classic example of what the Bible calls a "hardened heart." The Lord desires that we have broken and contrite spirits, in which we learn finally to bow in humble submission to his will. A person with a hardened heart stubbornly refuses to submit to that will. There is in Saul a deepening rebellion, a perseverance in his willfulness that causes his evil to become more organized and more difficult to turn away from. No longer do we see a spear-throwing episode in a moment of uncontrolled fury; instead, there are carefully planned attacks that involve the organization of three thousand soldiers!

Now imagine you are the narrator of this drama, and the story is being made into a TV miniseries. The director is discussing with you what scene should be shot next. "Let's see now, we've done the episode of the 'good lad beats the big, bad giant.' That will appeal to the youngsters. Then we had the 'romance and royal wedding number.' We'll get great ratings from the women viewers on that one. Then there was the one on 'the celebrated war hero becomes a fugitive on the run.' The action and adventure types will go for that. Oh yeah, and remember the psychological profile we did of 'the neurotic king eaten up with envy'? All the public television fans will like that one. Next was the 'massacre at Nob.' Oh brother, I bet we'll hear from ten different nationalities, all complaining that they are being unfavorably portrayed through Doeg. Now couldn't you write in a chase scene, you know, like in *The French Connection* or somethin'?"

We are about to embark on a breathless "Big Chase" that rivals any Hollywood production. For all practical appearances, the entire scene looks as if it will turn into a hands-down win for King Saul, with three thousand men at his command. David is a hunted fugitive, a leader of a ragtag band of six hundred malcontents. Finding and decimating him should be a cakewalk.

Except that God is with David.

A CONTEST OF WILLS

What is intriguing to observe in this story is that Saul was convinced that this was a power struggle between him and David over who would be king. On the other hand, David was resolute that he would never lay a hand on Saul—God's anointed king. Indeed, David's *biggest* challenge was how to avoid killing Saul and yet remain alive! However, what Saul did not realize was that his protagonist was really God himself. This story invites us to reflect upon the absolute futility of opposing God. In this case, it was a contest between the relentless but loving will of God and the diseased but powerful will of King Saul.

There is always a purpose to what our Creator does, even in the granting of power, and his will cannot ultimately be overruled. Yet Saul would spend his whole life as king seeking to have things his way. And that is the real issue here—whether we will choose to align ourselves with the will of God, or whether we will insist on going our own way.

David was willing to entrust himself to the will of God. Saul, on the other hand, would not bow fully to God's authority. Thus Saul's every desperate move to eliminate the threat of David was countered by the powerful resolve of the Lord. Of course, the players in this drama did not realize what we know—that Saul is actually the one in a no-win battle.

WHAT IS REBELLION?

When we see the futility and self-destruction that results from rebelling against God, it forces us to ask: What does rebellion actually mean?

Rebellion is essentially refusing to let God be God. To rebel against God is to serve an idol, to place something else in the supreme place that is God's alone. What we choose as our authoritative center is self instead of God. Whether our focus is on knowledge, power, wealth, or fame, etc., isn't so important. These attachments reveal that we are self-ruled people.

Anyone who truly takes God seriously, who believes God to be who he says he is, will be committed to the process of learning to submit and obey. To set one's own ideas above God's revealed Word means we really don't believe his Word to be true. To seek one's own will as Saul did entails a belief that one's own ideas are actually better than those of God.

Rebellion is also a failure to love God first and best and to love our neighbor as ourselves. That was Saul's predicament—he failed to acknowledge and love God as God. Yet we must wonder, as we watch Saul choose to live outside of reality and sink more and more into his own self-obsessed concerns, were there signs that he refused to read that would have revealed he was on the wrong path? What characterizes one centered in the self instead of in God?

Now let's look at the Big Chase that began at Keilah in 1 Samuel 23 to see the evidence and fruit of a man in rebellion.

SELF-DECEPTION RESISTS THE FACTS

After he had the priests of Nob and their families murdered, Saul heard that David and his men had gone to the Judean town of Keilah. In his demented thinking, the king believed that God was allowing him to capture David within the town's walls. "God has handed him over to me, for David has imprisoned himself by entering a town with gates and bars."

David was in Keilah because he was willing to postpone his flight from Saul in order to help his own people fight their enemy, the Philistines. After the victory in battle, David heard that Saul was planning to come to Keilah. So he asked the Lord two questions: "Will Saul come down, as your servant has heard?" And, "Will the citizens of Keilah surrender me to him?" When David learned that the answer was yes on both counts, he and his men fled to the hills. Once Saul heard that, he called off his expedition.

Even in this first episode of the chase scene, we see the outworking of the rebellion that so characterized Saul's self-deception. Imagine how Saul's reasoning must have sounded to his troops: "Come on, men, hurry up! I've just located the man who defeated the Philistines and made Israel a safer place for us and our children. Let's go find him and kill him!" Such was the nature of Saul's rebellion, a perspective so centered in self-deception that he would justify anything to create his own reality in order to accomplish his purposes.

LOTS OF GOD-TALK, BUT NO PRAYER

It's interesting to note how little Saul prays. When he heard David was in Keilah, he didn't pray; he just assumed that because Keilah was a walled city, David could be easily captured. Saul reasoned that God was on his side, and one thing that strengthened Saul's deception was his use of God-talk. "God has handed him over to me."

The more Saul slipped away from reality, the more he engaged in God-talk. He was quick to read God's favor into his behavior and to communicate that favor prematurely—without ever consulting God! But things never turned out as Saul expected. As much as Saul insisted that God was in agreement with him, there was never any such evidence. That should have given him pause. But Saul was totally consumed with his own wishes.

DISREGARD FOR HUMAN LIFE

Saul became increadingly calloused. He used people and casually disposed of them. He set out to destroy the village without blinking an eye the minute he heard that the Keilahites had been helped by David. At least in Nob there was evidence that one priest had helped David. But this time no one had helped David; it was *David* who helped the villagers! How could Saul have considered that a betrayal? Had he learned nothing from the horrors of Nob?

In organizing a huge troop movement to capture and kill a man who had just protected Israel, Saul also disregarded his own soldiers' safety. This kind of hard-core disregard for people is typical of a person obsessed with the pursuit of his will over God's.

FAILURE TO CARRY OUT PUBLIC DUTIES

How often we have heard it said in political discussion that it really doesn't matter what an elected official does in private; the only thing that matters is how he or she does the job. But the Bible recognizes no difference between public and private morality. We are whole people, and when we blatantly sin in a private area, it will eventually show up in the public arena as well.

In the beginning, Saul's sin against David was private. Only the narrator and the reader know about it. However, Saul's private sin had enormous public consequences for the nation of Israel. So long as Saul was occupied in seeking David's life, the Philistines continued their aggression without opposition. Israel's national security was threatened time and again. Saul's soldiers risked their lives on one wild goose chase after another, and the king's public policies became increasingly unjust and unstable, as events in both Nob and Keilah revealed.

Therefore, it shouldn't surprise us when we are told that there were many people "who were in distress or in debt or discontented." Nor should it surprise us that these discontented ones eventually chose to follow David as their leader, for David represented to them the bright hope of a new Israel. Their frustration was deeper than a mere quarrel between the poor, the politically marginalized, and the privileged landed gentry that Saul represented. They knew that something was "rotten in Denmark" when an army had to be formed because a mad king was attacking a hero, a true loyalist like David. Perhaps David's men might have responded as the World War II resistance fighters did in the film *The Sorrow and the Pity*. When asked if they felt like heroes for fighting in the right cause, the fighters replied, "We weren't heroes. We were just maladjusted enough to know something was very, very wrong, and we had to do something."

What was so very wrong at Keilah was that Saul, in his unrelenting rebellion against God, never thought to ask why God did not do what Saul expected there. The fact that nothing ever seemed to work in his favor should have said to Saul that he was desperately going down the wrong path. But he did not ask such questions because he did not want to know the truth. Such is the nature of rebellion.

THE DESERT OF ZIPH

With constant pressure from Saul, David and his men were forced to hide in the desolate areas of the mountains of Ziph, which belonged to Judah. Even though Saul was probably unfamiliar with those bleak hills, he would not be deterred. He still gathered up his army and set out to find David. "Day after day Saul searched for him, but God did not give David into his hands." Even with the aid of three thousand soldiers and solid intelligence reports, without *God's* intelligence working for him, Saul could not close in. David might as well have been in Tahiti.

There was a problem, however. Although the citizens there were of David's tribe, the Ziphites remained loyal to the king and informed Saul of David's whereabouts. They probably hoped to profit in some way from their betrayal of David. Then in a classic example of psychological projection coupled with more God-talk, Saul told the Ziphites, "The Lord bless you for your concern for me. . . . Find out where David usually goes and who has seen him there. They tell me he is very crafty."

Saul eventually tracked David down to a particular hill in the Desert of Maon. Saul and his men scurried up the hill while David and his men, in a desperate effort to escape, scurried down. But just as Saul's men were closing in for the capture, the king received a report from home. It was the one message, perhaps the *only* message that could have stopped him. "Come quickly! The Philistines are raiding the land." The message to Saul was unmistakable: don't allow your personal feud to come before the nation's security! This time he listened, and for the time being, David was safe again.

EXPERIENCE DOES NOT LIE

I asked before if there were signs of self-deception that Saul refused to heed. After the experience at Keilah and Ziph, he should have asked himself, *What do my repeated failures at trying to harm David mean? What am I to learn from this?* God gives us many chances to learn. Even if we refuse to listen to the probing of conscience, the experience of life alone should teach us what is right and what is wrong. C. S. Lewis once wrote, "What I like about experience is that it is such an honest thing . . .you may have deceived yourself, but experience is not trying to deceive you. The universe rings true wherever you fairly test it." Saul should have been able to test his universe and figure out that he and his kingdom were in jeopardy.

If Saul had done even a quick review of his experiences in his rebellious frame of mind, he might have reasoned like this: "Let's see now, every time I threw my spear at that son of Jesse, I missed. But I always was a lousy shot. And every time I sent David into battle against the Philistines, he was victorious. But David always was lucky. I tried to kill him in his sleep, but my own daughter Michal helped him sneak out the window. That girl—always falling for a handsome face. I never could get her to mind me. I sent my men to kill him when he hid out at Samuel's, but they fell down and started prophesying. Then I went to take care of the job myself. Lo and behold if I didn't do the same thing! Boy, I'm gonna check with the cook. It must have been something we ate.

"Then that no-good priest gave him bread and the sword. And it was ceremonial bread at that. That must have *really* ticked off Yahweh! Well, all right, I guess Doeg did get a little carried away when he murdered everyone, but do you know how it feels to finally find someone who supports me, *just because he cares?* I tell you, nobody knows the trouble I've seen.

"Then those Keilahites (God bless them!)—they were willing to surrender that son of Jesse to me even after he helped them win the battle against the Philistines! Man, talk about a crass and calculated PR move on his part, but I think the Keilahites saw through his deviousness. What a shame he got away before we could find him.

"When we heard where he was hiding out, three thousand of us could not find him! But then those loyal and faithful Ziphites came to me with information. But wouldn't you know, just as we were closing in on him, those despicable Philistines began attacking, and we had to leave. We were *that* close."

The point is that Saul had every opportunity to learn from his experiences. An honest examination of his own torment, anxiety, and repeated failure at trying to harm David should have been enough to convict him. His significant relationships were broken. His only allies were unsavory strangers like Doeg or citizens who told him what he wanted to hear because they feared for their safety. His leadership was pathetic and weak and his country in shambles. But instead of learning from his experience and repenting, Saul blamed and accused everyone who stood in his way. Ralph Waldo Emerson said that "people seem not to see that their opinion of the world is also a confession of character." Saul's perspective of the way things were revealed that he was a man of abysmal character on the brink of spiritual disaster.

The trouble was that Saul would not bend. He had to do things his way or no way at all. Saul was the ultimate control freak, but his insistence upon control at any price pushed him *out of control* and out of the parameters of God's will and protection.

SHOWDOWN AT EN GEDI (1 SAMUEL 24)

En Gedi was the last and most poignant part of the Big Chase. Just as soon as Saul dealt with the Philistines, he was back in hot pursuit of David. He tracked David from the village, to the wilderness, and even to the mountain where David and his men hid. How could he get so close and still miss? Abruptly we are told that "a cave was there, and Saul went in to relieve himself. David and his men were far back in the cave."

For the first time in this remarkable story, Saul was the one in the vulnerable position. And he didn't even know it. David's men encouraged him to take Saul's life, believing it was an opportunity granted from God. The men urged David saying, "This is the day the Lord spoke of when he said to you, 'I will will give your enemy into your hands for you to deal with as you wish.'" Whether the Lord really said this is questionable. However, David still refused to harm God's anointed king. But he did secretly creep up on Saul and cut off a portion of the king's robe. Yet even that act caused David to be filled remorse, perhaps because it brought shame and embarrassment to the king. When Saul walked away from the cave, finally David stood before him and spoke to him face to face, something he had not done since he fled from the royal court.

David cried out, proclaiming his innocence and showing Saul the piece of robe he had cut off. "This day you have seen with your own eyes how the Lord delivered you into my hands in the cave. Some urged me to kill you, but I spared you; I said, 'I will not lift my hand against my master, because he is the Lord's anointed.'" David asked for the pursuit to stop and to be cleared of all charges of treason. He wanted to be vindicated and found righteous. He did not ask for the crown, nor would he take any active role in securing the crown. That was God's gift and no one's inalienable right.

"May the Lord judge between you and me," David continued. "And may the Lord avenge the wrongs you have done to me, but my hand will not touch you. As the old saying goes, 'From evildoers come evil deeds,' so my hand will not touch you."

Now Saul had to respond. But before he could give David the answer to his precise question, he broke down in vulnerability and pathos: "Saul lifted up his voice and wept." He wept because he was now faced with the truth he had tried so terribly hard to avoid—that David would prevail. He wept because he was also faced with the fact of his own willful life. He wept because his life had gone so awry. And he wept because he was so very tired. Saul behaved like a beaten man who wanted out of the whole mess. And we weep with him at a life so full of promise that turned out to be so empty of possibilities.

When Saul finally regained his composure, he called David by his name for the first time in a long time: "Is that your voice, David, my son?" He conceded to David, "You are more righteous than I. You have treated me well, but I have treated you badly." And then the words we have waited to hear finally came: "I know that you will surely be king and that the kingdom of Israel will be established in your hands." This was a critical acknowledgment because unless Saul accepted David's right to the future, Israel would have no peace. So long as Saul kept up his insane pursuit, he jeopardized Israel's security against her enemies. His cry to David was, "Now swear to me by the Lord that you will not cut off my descendants or wipe out my name from my father's family." Thus, in their final moments together Saul begged David not to allow him to be lost to history. David gave his oath to Saul that that would not happen, and then David returned home.

Yet, unbelievably, Saul *continued* to pursue David. The future king was neither free nor safe, even though Saul knew the truth of God's plan for the kingdom. His intent was still to thwart that plan. The question is why?

THE IRRATIONALITY OF REBELLION

Why did Saul continue to behave in such self-destructive ways? Because his heart was hard. His was a case of the "stiff neck," for he would not bow to anyone's rules but his own. With all the personal tragedy and national damage that his rebellion caused, it made absolutely no sense that he persisted in pursuing David. But then again, Saul was much like a child when it came to insisting on his way.

What parents have not at times shaken their heads over a child's headstrong attempts to disobey? Whether it's the near-comic picture of a two-year-old's jaw jutted out saying "No!" or the sad prospect of a teenager making heartbreaking choices, the human will is at work in defiant, destructive, and irrational ways. And Saul's will was working overtime!

Why did Saul behave as he did, especially when his confession to David revealed that he knew in his deepest self he was wrong? He even acknowledged that he knew David was God's next choice as king. How could someone believe in an all-powerful God and yet stand against God's plan? Wouldn't a reasonable man bow to the reality he knew in his heart was true? When Saul saw God's consistent protection of David, why didn't Saul align himself with God's purposes, instead of insisting on his own will?

It must have taken a great deal of energy for Saul to keep from looking at the truth. To recognize that David's triumphs were due to God's favor and yet to try feverishly to eliminate God's man was insane. Surely Saul had to silence his inner voice of conscience. Then he had to silence every other voice that spoke the truth to him. Sadly, Saul did far more than violate his conscience. He did great harm to David and even to his own children, tormented himself and his kingdom, lost the respect of almost everyone, destroyed his monarchy, and muddied his reputation in history. He did all this in an attempt to fight what he knew all along was a *fait accompli*.

That is the madness and frustration of rebellion. It is the ultimate in irrationality. Which is why we can never really pin sin down. No matter how much effort we invest, it will always remain to some extent unexplainable, because inherent in sin is the denial of truth. As Tom Peter writes: "We cover our unwholesome motives and violent acts against others with a veneer of goodness. We sugarcoat our garbage." (*Radical Evil in Soul and Society*) Why do we do this? Because those in rebellion have a stake in hiding the truth of their sin. It was the height of irrationality for Saul to fight David, for in doing so, he was fighting God. But what is even more amazing to ponder is that Saul knew it but did it anyway.

That is the heart of rebellion: to know the truth, to see God's will, and yet refuse to submit to it.

WHAT TO DO ABOUT REBELLION

Remember Whose Will Counts

As we watch the effects of Saul's rebellion, we are taught several lessons about the futility of fighting God. Saul failed to learn the first and most essential lesson of human history: The world is not centered around our wills, but rather around the will of God. The price we pay will be enormous if we refuse to accept and live in that reality.

Saul was a textbook case of rebellion—someone who would not relinquish control and who seemed to insist on his right to be wrong! Whereas David revealed a life centered in God and submissive to the will of God, Saul's life was entirely self-centered. These texts in Samuel speak volumes about the better path to take.

Remember That Sin Snowballs

By this point in the story Saul was no longer guilty of a single sin such as envy or hate. His steady choices had led him down a path that was so choked with unrepented sin that it was nearly impossible to reverse.

By the end of this episode, we will see Saul a beaten man who seems to want out of the struggle. But it is too late. Events were set in motion that Saul could not stop even if he had wanted to. Of course he could have repented at any point, and his sins would have been for-given. But there is always the juncture where the price of sin must be paid, even after it has been confessed.

Remember the Impact One Choice Can Make

There is a third lesson the narrator of Samuel wishes his readers to understand: Our choices have enormous impact on others. An assassin's bullet killed Israel's prime minister Yitzhak Rabin. But the consequence of one zealot pulling a trigger wasn't just the death of an important leader. One man's action left a wife without a husband, children without their father, grandchildren without their grandfather, a country without its talented prime minister, and a world without the benefit of this important elder statesman. The assassin's bullet did not just change one man's destiny, it changed the destiny of the whole world. So do our lives—and the choices we make—have a ripple effect.

The lives of David and Saul too reflect how profoundly each man was affected by the other's choices. David spent at least twelve years running from Saul. Through the process he learned tactical wisdom, developed enormous leadership skills and political savvy, and developed godly character. God used all of Saul's harassment and sin against David to make David into his man.

Saul was equally affected by David's choices to live for God. He suffered enormous frustration and exhaustion at not being able to harm David. Saul experienced the pain of rejection when his children chose David over their father. He lost the throne. But unlike David, he did not learn from the difficult circumstances because of his hardened rebellion against God. Trapped in his own self-centeredness, the king self-destructed.

THERE'S NO OVERRIDING GOD'S WILL

If the life and reign of Saul teaches us anything, it is that no human choice can alter reality. Yes, the Creator has given us a will and limited freedom to make choices that are significant. And we may choose to use our freedom constructively or destructively. But even the sinful use of freedom cannot ultimately alter God's purposes. The more Saul continued to attack David, the more apparent was the plan, the purpose, and the divine will operating behind every event. Saul could not thwart God's plan. Indeed, God used even Saul's sin to accomplish his purposes. Human rebellion can do tragic harm to its carrier and to others. But there is nothing that can ultimately overturn the will of God.

There was only one way out for Saul. He had to admit he was wrong and return to square one. It was not possible for him to get back into God's will without radical repentance. C. S. Lewis put it this way in *The Great Divorce:* "I do not think that all who choose wrong roads perish; but their rescue consists in being put back on the right road. A wrong sum can be put right: but only by going back till you find the error and working it afresh from that point, never by simply *going on.* Evil can be undone, but it cannot 'develop' into good. Time does not heal it."

As we read the book of Samuel, we long for Saul to learn from his errors. We want him to be able to say, as Estella says in Charles Dickens's *Great Expectations,* "I have been bent and broken, but I hope into a better shape." Yet for Saul that moment never seemed to come. His rebellion made him insist the world be identified with his will and not God's. He lived increasingly in his own little corner of unreality, blind to himself, unloving and hateful toward others, and worse, defiant toward God.

QUESTIONS AND REFLECTIONS

1. What picture or feeling comes to your mind when you hear the word *repent?*

2. What are the consequences, the results, when we fail to line our lives up with reality (God)?

3. What in your life needs to be more in alignment with God's ways? Identify some practical steps you might take.

4. What was it that made you face the truth about your failure to walk in God's ways?

5. What devices did you use to cover the problem?

6. How did God help you to overcome a vice? What role did your own obedience play?

C h a p t e r
E i g h t

Submission:
The Remedy for Rebellion

I know a man who is an atheist and proud of it. He told me once, "I'm just a maverick. I have a mind of my own, and I don't let others direct my course of action. I love my freedom, and I'm not about to take orders from some supposed 'father in heaven.'"

"I'm curious. Do you raise your children with the same philosophy?" I asked.

"Absolutely!" he answered. "I give my teenage daughters lots of love and space. I tell them they may choose whatever path they feel suits them best. It's their decision how to live their lives, but I'll be there to support them."

A few years later I attended the funeral of his eighteen-year-old daughter. Brilliant, gifted, she had enrolled in her first year of college—and now she was dead from a drug overdose.

As I walked out of the funeral service, I saw her father. I don't think I have ever seen grief as deeply etched in a human face. I walked over to comfort him, but all I could do was weep with him. He said to me, "She had everything in the world to live for. It was hers for the taking. I gave her love and the freedom to choose. But why couldn't she see that doing drugs was killing her? What good is freedom if it leads you to the grave?"

Rarely have I heard someone state so concisely the results of the tragic misuse of human choice. We think to be free means doing it our way. God says true freedom comes from doing it his way. And the fruit that is produced by living in harmony with God is not death but all the things that pertain to life: joy and peace and knowledge and power.

C. S. Lewis put it this way in *The Great Divorce:* "There are only two kinds of people in the end: those who say to God, 'Thy will be done,' and those to whom God says in the end, 'Thy will be done.'"

Saul has shown us the terrifying results of using our freedom to choose independence from God. By contrast, David shows us that there is a better way to live our lives, and that better way is in obedience and surrender to God. As we will see in the next chapter, David's performance during the wilderness years was not flawless. Yet, considering the enormous pressure he was under, it is amazing that he was able to lead his men so wisely in the middle of such stupendous crises. How did he do it?

For all of David's passion, giftedness, exuberance, and charisma, there was something far deeper still that operated in and through his personality. He truly loved God, and he expressed his love by submitting to God's authority. It is no small thing to consider that a man so compelling, so forceful, and so engaging chose to submit to God's rule. Yes, David made big mistakes, but he always recognized he was the creature who must submit to God the Creator.

HOLINESS

What is the fruit of a life submitted to God? We become like him! One of God's goals is to shape our character so that we will manifest his kindness, mercy, love, purity, wisdom, and so on, in ways that are reflected through our own distinctive personalities. To put it another way, God is making us holy. But there is a requirement in learning how to submit to God's authority: humility. We won't get very far in the development of holiness if we are defensive about our flaws. That is why truly holy people are so easy to be with. They have been around God too long to try to pretend they are perfect. They are the first to acknowledge their pride and their faults.

Then why are holy people so joyful and radiant? One reason is that they know the answer to their character problem doesn't reside in them but with God. They don't try to please God through the efforts of the flesh, such as moralism or legalism, but by their obedient walk in the Spirit. They know a surrendered life comes by listening to God, walking in step with him. As Leanne Payne writes, "Only in union with him, listening to him and carrying out his orders are we holy. . . . To preach the law apart from teaching the walk in the Spirit leaves the flock with what they ought to do, yet without the power to do it." (*Listening Prayer*)

Holiness comes from knowing that obedience must arise out of communion with God, who will give us everything we need. It also comes from committing our wills wholeheartedly to obeying God's commands. David was absolutely committed to learning how to live in step with God. No one loved the law of God like David. But it was his intimate walk with God in the Spirit—and the lessons learned in adversity—that gave him the power to live it out.

David lived in the presence of God. As he drew close to God—walking with him, talking with him, asking for his help—God's character began to rub off on David. We watch as God begins to soften David's will, making him thirsty for righteousness, restraining and correcting his hot-blooded temper and giving him the courage to choose the good. David's life reveals that holiness is a by-product of a Spirit-led, obedient walk with God.

THE SURRENDERED LIFE IS . . .

Just as Saul's life revealed a pattern of choosing self over God, so David's life revealed a pattern of submission, a willingness to learn God's ways and seek to please him.

There are two common misunderstandings about learning God's ways. First, some think that converting to faith in Christ automatically means we know everything about God's ways. David had a passionate faith in the true God, but David had to learn how to listen to God, how to please him, and walk in his ways. Learning how to live in submission to God is a process. And God is usually far more patient about our learning curve than we (and other people) are. Second, we feel that if we could just get away to a quiet desert, away from interruptions and pressures, we could learn what we need to know so much faster. But David's learning took place right in the midst of the difficulties of life, not apart from them. David often learned his greatest lessons about God when he was under the greatest pressure.

Although the German philosopher Nietzsche was not a Christian, he coined a phrase that is helpful in understanding the nature of discipleship. He said that discipleship is a "long obedience in the same direction." David learned some valuable lessons in his long obedience that can greatly benefit us. For example, when we are under stress and trying to be faithful, what are the pitfalls to avoid?

DON'T ACT BEFORE YOU PRAY! (1 SAMUEL 21–22)

One of the easiest things to do when the pressure is mounting is to act before we pray. We tend to think of David as a man of action. But most often even in the midst of extreme anger, David prayed before he made a move. However, as his flight from Saul began, it seems that David acted impetuously and escaped to Philistine country before he prayed.

David's flight from Saul began in earnest after he arrived in Nob and received the bread of the Presence and Goliath's sword from the priest Ahimelech. Knowing that Saul was after his life, and knowing he was now branded as a fugitive and an outlaw, he sought refuge in the Philistine city of Gath. That David would go to Philistine country—even to Goliath's native city—revealed how extreme he felt his situation was. David visited Achish, the king of Gath. His intent apparently was to go incognito, but he seriously underestimated his fame, as the king's servants immediately recognized him.

David was justifiably terrified that Achish recognized him as well. This meant he was in an even more vulnerable position, for it would make him a threat to his own nation as well as a valuable hostage. If David had a plan, it was destroyed, for now he had to escape from both Saul *and* Achish.

The great warrior and future king of Israel was in a jam. So, with characteristic quick-wittedness, he tried to convince Achish that he was harmless by playing insane. In a far cry from any royal demeanor, he threw himself on the floor and let spittle run down from his mouth onto his beard. The theatrics worked. In a wonderful scene, Achish, a busy king with plenty of his own political headaches to occupy the day, acted like any CEO at a board meeting. He took one look at this drooling madman, turned to his advisors, and in effect said: "Whaaaat?? Do you think I'm running short on imbeciles? Get him outta here!" David's deception was successful, and he escaped from Gath.

Did David really think he could travel into Philistine country unnoticed? He was a Jew with an enormous reputation, carrying a gigantic sword! There is a scene in the comedy film *Sister Act* that reminds me of David's situation. When the Mother Superior turns to the nuns, all dressed in full habits and about to disperse into a Las Vegas casino to look for a kidnapped woman, she advises, "Just try to blend in." David had about as much hope of blending in with the Philistines as those nuns did in Las Vegas.

As funny as David's episode in Gath reads, one can hardly believe it was fun for David to live through. He wrote about it in Psalm 34, and we are given an extraordinary glimpse into not only what he was feeling but how he interpreted his narrow escape. In the midst of what must have been sheer terror, David begins: "I will extol the Lord at all times; his praise will always be on my lips. My soul will boast in the Lord; let the afflicted hear and rejoice. Glorify the Lord with me; let us exalt his name together. I sought the Lord, and he answered me; he delivered me from all my fears. Those who look to him are radiant; their faces are never covered with shame. This poor man called, and the Lord heard him; he saved him out of all his troubles. The angel of the Lord encamps around those who fear him, and he delivers them. Taste and see that the Lord is good; blessed is the man who takes refuge in him."

This is no spiritual pearl from our beloved but slightly senile Sunday school teacher. This comes from a man on the run, whose very life hung in the balance and who had every reason to feel desperate and be full of self-pity.

It is obvious from the psalm that David prayed once he was *in* this mess. But there is no mention in the text that he had prayed before he went. It is hard to imagine that God would have guided him to seek refuge in Philistine territory. Still the message is comforting that even when our troubles are due to our own impetuosity, we can still cry out to God in prayer, and he will hear and answer and deliver us.

DON'T FORGET YOUR GOD-GIVEN RESPONSIBILITIES (1 SAMUEL 23)

We may think that when the pressure is the worst, we might be excused from our duties and responsibilities. But David shows us otherwise. Having narrowly escaped from Philistine country, he gathered his men, and they found temporary refuge in the hills of the Judean wilderness. But when David heard that the Philistines were attacking the Judean town of Keilah, he asked God if he should help the embattled villagers. Of course, coming into a town would make him more visible, easier for Saul to find. David was understandably nervous.

It says a great deal about David's character that he would even consider helping his countrymen when at the time he was fleeing for his own life. He asked the Lord if he should rescue the villagers from the Philistine raiders, and God directed him to do it. However, David's own men were nervous; it would be easy for Saul to track them there. Therefore, David went back to the Lord to check his guidance once more. Again, God commanded him to attack the Philistines. And under God's direction, there was a great victory.

While Saul by now seemed to have little regard for human life, David demonstrated both a strong sense of duty and compassion. Indeed David's conflict was over how to help one group of people, the Keilahites, and how to still protect his own men. Submission to God meant recognizing his duty and having compassion for his people before worrying about his own self-interests. In difficult times that is hard to do.

DON'T RESIST GOD'S COMFORT

In times of crisis it is tempting to withdraw from God and from people and sit in our misery alone. We must remember that not only has God not forgotten us, but he wants to reach out to us if only we will let him.

It was a very low time for David when he escaped to the wilderness of Ziph. David had just been informed that Saul had successfully located the general area where he and his men were hiding. Furthermore, he heard that Saul had every intention to murder him. But while Saul and his three thousand soldiers were not able to find David's *exact* location, Jonathan had no problem getting through to his friend and helping him "find strength in God."

Jonathan told David, "Don't be afraid. My father Saul will not lay a hand on you." Then Jonathan made two startling statements: "You will be king over Israel, and I will be second to you. Even my father Saul knows this." Jonathan had never before been so explicit about his growing conviction that Yahweh had transferred the kingdom from his father to David. He was officially renouncing his claim to the throne, without bitterness or jealousy, and accepting a subordinate role to David as his second in command.

With his mission accomplished—having reminded David that he was the future king who was beloved by God—Jonathan prepared to leave. As he and David had done so many times in the past, they made a covenant together before the Lord, not realizing that this would be the last time they would ever see each other because Jonathan would be killed in battle.

David would never again have a friend like Jonathan. The fact that he listened to and was restored by his friend's bold reminders tells us that the future king's life would be much poorer without Jonathan.

GOD'S GIFT FOR GOD'S PEOPLE

We have seen how to avoid some of the obstacles in our walk of obedience. What are the resources we can use to help us align our will with God's will? David shows us three things: maintain a vital prayer life, choose godly friends, and know how to wait on God. Let's examine David's prayer life first.

PRAYER

The Psalms and 1 and 2 Samuel reveal much about David's prayer life. He and the Lord talked as two good friends, in easy trust. David poured his heart out to God and held nothing back. We hear frequently today that we must be "in touch with our feelings." Though we may inwardly groan over such an overused phrase, there *is* wisdom in being able to identify strong emotions. To not know when we are angry or afraid, for example, gives such emotions greater power over us. But what we seldom hear addressed is what we are supposed to do with these emotions once we have correctly identified them. David wasn't merely a man "in touch" with his emotions. He knew what to do with them—he poured them out to God in prayer! When David was angry, he let it fly. When he wondered why God was taking so long to rescue him from his enemies, he complained loudly, "O Lord, how long will you look on? Rescue my life from their ravages, my precious life from these lions." (Ps. 35:17) When those he trusted betrayed him, he cried out to God for comfort, and sometimes even for vengeance. "May all who gloat over my distress be put to shame and confusion; may all who exalt themselves over me be clothed with shame and disgrace." (Ps. 35:26)

David shows us that a life yielded to God's will is never sterile and void of passion, as David's life demonstrates. Through David's prayers and actions we see a loving and passionate relationship to God, not a sterile account of a distant God who drops a law book from on high and shouts, "Follow these rules and, for crying out loud, stay out of trouble!" David's life is a story of a God who gets down into the trenches with his people, who loves them profoundly, and who isn't caught off guard when they blow it.

HONESTY WITH GOD

Nor does a prayerfully surrendered life mean we pray with pious platitudes. In fact, if David's prayers teach us anything, it is that we must not deny our true feelings as we pray. David was so devastatingly honest about his emotions, his prayers were so real that they are uncomfortable for those wanting to come to God all dressed up in their Sunday best. Anyone feeling that the problem with Christianity is that it requires a fake smile and a phony optimism should read Psalms to stand corrected. David's example utterly defeats our tendency to try being holy without first being human.

But David did something more important than merely expressing his feelings in prayer. He reflected on his deepest feelings *right in front of God*. He wept, complained, and paraded his problems in front of a Comforter who he knew cared about every detail of his misery. David's posture was always of the one in need addressing the only One who has the resources to help. Such raw candor never left him in narcissistic self-pity, or despair, though his prayers often expressed immense pain. Instead, his pain was nearly always transformed into praise. How did that happen?

FROM PAIN TO PRAISE

David refused to deny either the depth of his pain or the possibility of its transformation into praise. As Kathleen Norris writes in *The Paradox of the Psalms*, "The psalms demand that we recognize that praise does not spring from a delusion that things are better than they are, but rather from the human capacity for joy." Perhaps better stated, praise springs from a human capacity for hope that leads to joy. David's ability to praise God in difficulties did not stem from naive optimism, but from a robust trust in a Creator who is passionately concerned and invested in his creation's welfare.

David's prayers show us that we should not rely on praise alone, nor should we idealize pain in our effort to know our Creator better. A devout Christian I recently met told me that "praise, once you really know God, is all there is." That sounds good and pious, but it is simply not true. The very real pain and suffering in life dramatically challenge her thesis. Shortly after meeting this woman, I met another Christian recovering from drug addiction, who told me essentially that pain was the avenue to really knowing God: "Being in touch with your pain, not hiding from it but owning it, that's what it's about." The second woman would no doubt look in disdain at the first one and say, "Honey, get real." The truth is that both pain and praise are part of the authentic Christian experience. David's prayers teach us that submission to God's plan requires honesty about both realities.

David was unrelenting in his realism about what he saw in himself and in life more generally. And that is the way we should be. Life is full of reasons to praise as well as to grieve. We must not deny the depth of our pain, but we must bring that pain into the very presence of a God who cares. This is the way to transform pain into praise. The example of David shows us that God wants from us so much more than polite correctness. He isn't interested in producing self-righteous experts who never make mistakes. Rather, God wants passionate lovers who obey his moral laws, not merely because it is our expected duty but because we have fallen in love with the Lawgiver himself!

PRAYER KEEPS US FROM DOING EVIL

Times of testing not only reveal what is in the heart of the one being tested, but also what is in the hearts of others. In times of crisis we may be deeply disappointed in people we thought we could count on. Yet we have been created to trust and be open. How was David able to overcome his disappointment in the people who let him down? What kept him from becoming bitter?

He prayed his hurt to God and asked God to heal it. David also turned over his anger and feelings of bitterness to God. He didn't spare God his rage or hurt. Doing this kept him from taking it out on others.

David also had a realistic assessment of life and people. The truth is that people will let us down, just as we will let others down. That is always painful. It would be an inconsolable grief if people were where we should place our trust. What enables us to remain open and trusting isn't our confidence that people are reliable but that God is.

SEEK WISE COUNSEL

To live a life in submission to God we need people who will speak the truth to us and faithfully uphold biblical standards. One of the great protections against deception or discouragement is objective counsel from someone in a position to point out our willfulness. It is to such a person that we should seek to become morally accountable. As we have seen, King Saul did not want the counsel of others. Far from it; when people disagreed with him, Saul either ignored them or killed them! He ignored Samuel's guidance and thus lost his counsel and support. Saul refused to listen to his children and thus lost their emotional support. Thinking the priests of Nob were co-conspirators with David, he killed them and thereby lost priestly assistance.

But David was the far better model. He listened to what Jonathan said, and through him he heard the voice of God. David was able to get his perspective in focus. Granted it is easier to hear positive truth, but throughout the book of Samuel, we see that David listened to painful truth too.

Through Jonathan especially we see how important it is that we have friends whose character has proved to be trustworthy, and whose counsel is wise. Cicero was correct that "they seem to take away the sun from the world who withdraw friendship from life." If David had lived today, he might easily have found friends who would say, "Listen, the only way to cope with so much professional and personal stress is to take up jogging, learn how be your own best friend, and promise you will establish better 'boundaries' the next time you engage in a ministry of music therapy to troubled leaders. Here's a twelve-step program with cassettes for your recovery." But Jonathan wisely directed David's attention away from his present troubles and toward the God who would provide for him and fortify him for duty.

Everyone has times when their calm trust is shattered, and David certainly went through those shattering times. But he was fortunate to have a wise friend to remind him of what he already knew but needed to hear again: God is in charge, and he is never taken by surprise at what assails us.

Friends may love us at all times, but they are especially helpful during times of great difficulty. Like David, we all need Jonathans during our times of spiritual trials, temptations, and failing faith. We need real friends to tell us the truth, to give us a healing word when our faith falters, and to help us recognize the hand of God when we are too embattled to see it.

LEARN TO WAIT ON GOD (1 SAMUEL 24)

David demonstrated that learning to wait on God is another aspect of a life lived in submission. The truth is, nobody likes to wait. Especially for people in modern western society, waiting is sometimes really an agony. We want our answers the way some of us want our food—fast. We wonder why God couldn't have just FAXed the answer to David! David had to learn how to wait, especially through his experience in En Gedi.

After David fled to the En Gedi desert, on the shore of the Dead Sea, Saul entered the very cave in which David and some of his men were hiding. It would have been the perfect chance to slay Saul, as many of David's men urged him to do. But David restrained his men and resisted the temptation. The point remained, no matter how easy it would have been to take matters into his own hands, David was willing to wait for God's solution to the problem. If Saul was to be punished, it was God's business to do it.

WAITING FOR GOD'S TIMING

David chose wisely to wait for God's solution to his problem. But why did Israel's future king have to do that when he could just as easily have resolved things for himself?

David answered this question in Psalm 62. He teaches us that there are enormous benefits to be gained by waiting on God. When we wait for God and fix our attention on him, we are reminded that he is the source of all life. "My soul finds rest in God alone; my salvation comes from him. He alone is my rock and my salvation; he is my fortress, I will never be shaken." Who are we to decide who lives or dies? Only God should do that.

Waiting for God also reminds us who is sovereign. It is God who takes initiative and orders the timing of events. There is a time for every purpose under heaven, and waiting for God reminds us that his timing is critical—and best. Waiting for God develops stability of character. Rather than fearing human pressures, we learn to be more serene and peaceful.

WAITING FOR GOD'S VINDICATION

Saul slandered David at every opportunity. The desire to go to the people and set the record straight must have been great. Yet, we do not have even one account of David rushing either to defend himself or to spill the dirt on Saul. Why wasn't David more worried about setting the record straight? Because he was content to let the truth come out in God's good time, and in his way. He did appeal to God for vindication, but only to God. By way of contrast, Saul talked to anyone who would listen. Anyone, that is, except God. It could well be said that when David was reviled, like Jesus, "He reviled not again, but entrusted himself to him who judges justly."

Charles Spurgeon wrote a powerful commentary on the Psalms. His analysis of slander from David's Psalm 120 is extraordinarily insightful. He said, "Slander occasions distress of the most grievous kind. Those who have felt the edge of a cruel tongue know assuredly that it is sharper than a sword. Calumny rouses our indignation by a sense of injustice, and yet we find ourselves helpless to fight the evil, or to act in our own defense. We could ward off the strokes of a cutlass, but we have no shield against a liar's tongue. We do not know who was the father of the falsehood, nor where it was born, nor where it has gone, nor how to follow it, nor how to stay its withering influence. We are perplexed and know not which way to turn. Like the plagues of flies in Egypt, it baffles opposition, and few can stand before it. Detraction touches us in the tenderest point, cuts to the quick, and leaves a venom behind which it is difficult to extract. . . . *Silence to man and prayer to God* are the best cures for the evil of slander." (my emphasis)

When David said, "I cried out to the Lord," it was the wisest course that he could follow. Spurgeon continues, "It is of little use to appeal to our fellows on the matter of slander, for the more we stir in it, the more it spreads; it is of no avail to appeal to the honor of the slanderers, for they have none, and the most piteous demands for justice will only increase their malignity and encourage them to issue fresh insult. To whom should children cry but to their father?"

When David wrote, "Deliver my soul, O Lord, from lying lips," Spurgeon offered this: "It will need divine power to save a man from these deadly instruments. . . . The soul, the life of a man, is endangered by lying lips. The faculty of speech becomes a curse when it is degraded into a mean weapon for smiting people behind their backs. We need to be delivered from slander by the Lord's restraint upon wicked tongues, or else be delivered out of it by having our good name cleared from the liar's calumny."

It would be impossible to underestimate the damage and evil that result from gossip and slander. The Scriptures couldn't be clearer: "For in the same way you judge others, you will be judged, and with the measure you use, it will be measured to you." (Matt. 7:2) Oswald Chambers says to the person who has "been shrewd in finding out the defects in others, remember that will be exactly the measure given to you. Life serves back the coin you pay." (*My Utmost for His Highest*) Jim Cymbala, the pastor of Brooklyn Tabernacle Church, said in an interview with *Leadership* magazine (1993) that what most sapped spiritual power in the church was grieving and quenching the Spirit's power through gossip and slander. He observed:

> Whenever we receive new members into the church, my final charge to them is, Never slander or gossip about another member. If you hear somebody talking about a person present, if you ever hear a critical word [about anyone], we charge you and authorize you to stop that person in their tracks. Say to them, Excuse me, has Pastor Cymbala hurt you? Has an usher hurt you? They'll apologize. Come with me right now to the pastor's office, or I'll make an appointment for you. The pastor will bring whoever hurt you, and if necessary they will kneel before you and apologize. But we won't permit talking behind their backs, slander or gossip.
>
> We can't be going to prayer meeting and calling on God, "Lord, come in power!" and then during the week be grieving the Holy Spirit by gossiping and phone calls. Of all the things that kill the Spirit's power in churches, it's talking.

Nevertheless, slander forces us to ask: Whose favor are we ultimately seeking—God's or man's? The desire to please people is a powerful impulse, but human approval can keep us from doing the right thing, the courageous thing. David knew that the answer did not lie in defending himself to others, or in leaking damaging reports on Saul. The only solace was to be found in God. His first and only response was to fix his total attention on God and wait for vindication.

WAITING FOR THE MOMENT OF TRUTH

David refused to publicly expose Saul in return for Saul's slander, but that does not mean he never spoke the truth. The incident in the cave in the Desert of Maon was a God-arranged moment that David did not let slip by. When Saul left the cave and was at a safe distance, David confronted him and was vigorous in his own defense. "He said to Saul, 'Why do you listen when men say, "David is bent on harming you"? This day you have seen with your own eyes how the Lord delivered you into my hands in the cave. Some urged me to kill you, but I spared you; I said, "I will not lift my hand against my master, because he is the Lord's anointed." . . . Against whom has the king of Israel come out? Whom are you pursuing? A dead dog? A flea? May the Lord be our judge and decide between us. May he consider my cause and uphold it; may he vindicate me by delivering me from your hand.'" In no uncertain terms, David told Saul he was not guilty of the things people said he was guilty of. David also reminded the king that no matter how much he remained silent, Saul continued to stalk him, slander him, and attempt to destroy him. What was Saul trying to accomplish?

David clearly believed that the power ultimately to transform his sorrowful situation lay not in violence toward Saul but in God's judgment and deliverance. However, submission to God did not mean that David had to passively accept Saul's abusive behavior. On the contrary, he fled from Saul to protect his life! David hated what Saul had done. He did not sentimentalize the treatment he suffered at the king's hand. But to fight back using Saul's weapons would have been to play with the devil's tools.

SUBMISSION TO GOD

We see through David's experience that as we learn to live in submission to God's will, we will also need to develop a certain detachment, a certain attitude that no longer sees people or jobs or even personal reputations as rights or possessions. Rather, they are gifts from God to be enjoyed while they last. Neither are we devastated if for a season they are taken away, for we must learn as David did that what matters to God has little to do with external realities. What matters most is living a life that is pleasing to God.

When Billy Graham spoke at President Nixon's funeral, he remarked that the older we get, the more we realize that what others think about us is of little importance. And the older we get, the clearer it becomes that the only opinion, the only judgment, that ultimately matters is *God's* opinion of us.

Recently I attended a worship service where I heard a remarkable story from the pulpit. There was an American soldier who was fighting overseas. A mail service existed that arranged for people to write to the soldiers to give them a moral boost. One day this soldier, whom we will call Sam, received a delightful letter from a woman in New York City. They began corresponding and found they had many things in common—for one, a shared Christian faith. He was amazed by how her letters always picked up his spirits. Being at war was a very lonely and difficult experience for him. But she encouraged him with biblical promises, or simply by saying that she prayed for him daily.

Eventually he came home on furlough. When he realized that he was going to have an afternoon in New York before flying out again, he decided to write her. He said that he would love to meet her and thank her in person for how much she'd encouraged him spiritually. He told her that he would be at Central Park, and where to look for him. She wrote back and said she would be wearing a red corsage on her dress so he could spot her easily.

Sam got to the park early and sat and read a paper. He scanned the vicinity to see if there were any women with a red carnation, and then he went back to his paper. Suddenly the most beautiful woman he had ever seen walked up to him, smiling. She was radiant, beautifully dressed, elegant and slim, and her voice was so kind and tender that his heart skipped a beat. He thought to himself, *If only the Lord would send a woman like that to me!* To his astonishment he heard the woman say to him, "Hi, soldier! Would you like to have some lunch? There's a marvelous restaurant right around the corner to your right." He glanced at his watch to see how much time he had before the rendezvous with the woman who had supported him in prayer. He still had five minutes, and he wanted desperately to go, even for just a cup of coffee.

But as he glanced up from his watch, he spotted an elderly woman across from him on another bench. She looked in her eighties, and had a weather-worn face that was deeply lined. She was dressed very poorly, an old black coat around a tattered dress. And in her coat lapel was a bright red carnation. His heart sank, and though he felt torn, he said to the beautiful blonde woman in front of him, "I would love to go, you have no idea how much. But I have a prior commitment. I owe a great deal to someone who has helped me through a difficult time, and I am not free to do anything else. But thank you with all my heart for inviting me."

She just smiled and said, "Well, if anything changes your mind, I'll be at the restaurant."

As she strode off he prayed, "Lord, sometimes I wish I didn't know so much about being obedient. Yet, as much as I want to go, if it was your will, you would have worked out the circumstances. So I will obey you and trust in your perfect plan for my life, even though I feel that perfection just walked by me."

He sighed and walked over to the elderly lady. Smiling at her and putting out his hand, he said, "I believe we have a lunch date today."

To his amazement she replied, "No, we don't. But I'll tell you who you *do* have one with. That lovely young lady who just came over to you pinned this red corsage on me. Then she pointed to you and told me that if that soldier sitting on the bench came over and offered to take me to lunch, I was supposed to tell you that *she* was the one you are really looking for. And she is waiting for you at the restaurant right around the corner to your right." He was bowled over, but started to sprint for the restaurant.

They had a glorious lunch, continued corresponding, and got married as soon as he was out of the army. How the pastor ended this story was very moving: "Don't underestimate God's goodness. He has your best interests at heart and he knows what he is doing. But usually we first have to learn the tough discipline of saying no to what we desperately want, so that it doesn't become an idol. Don't assume that what you want and what God wants for your life may be all that different. Maybe he will give you what you want. But he will not give the gift before you learn relinquishment. If he doesn't give you what you thought you needed, then trust that he has something much better and more suitable for you. Don't resist obedience, and don't believe God will always be on the opposite side of your wishes! Trust his goodness and obey him no matter how much it hurts at the time. Then see what a glorious future he has for you!"

A yielded life is a life that cares about and lives for God's opinion. This was the way David lived his life. It was a life that joyfully recognized, whether in times of blessing or suffering, that the only safety we can know is in trusting, obeying, and surrendering our lives to the Living God.

QUESTIONS AND REFLECTIONS

1. What picture comes to mind when you hear a person described as holy?

2. To what sins do you become vulnerable when you are under stress? What can you do to correct this problem?

3. How can you pray with greater honesty to God?

4. Have you ever used Psalms to pray your hurt, anger, or fear to God? If so, how did it help?

5. What role have godly friends played in your life when you were in difficulty?

6. How has waiting for God's answer for a situation, rather than moving on your own timetable, made a positive difference in your life? What difficulties did you experience in waiting?

7. What lessons have you learned about how to deal with slander?

8. How can we build our confidence that God desires to give us what is best for us?

Chapter Nine

Anger:
A Force That Must Be
Reckoned With

I traveled by plane recently, and I sat down next to a distraught mother of a four-year-old. The child was insisting on having her own way. "Fasten your seat belt, sweetheart. We're almost ready to take off."

"No!" she shouted emphatically.

"Please don't yell because there are other people on the plane. Here's your juice—this will make you feel better," the mother cajoled.

"No!" the child yelled. Then she stood up on her seat.

Her mother told her, "Sit back down, *now.*"

"No!" the little girl insisted.

"Don't tell me no. When I say to sit down, I mean sit down!"

By this time the mother was obviously embarrassed by this public confrontation. The child just stared out the window, mute. "Did you hear me?" the mother asked with great intensity.

"But I want to watch the people!" the child responded in tearful rage.

An ensuing argument lasted almost five minutes, with the mother increasingly more desperate and the child more angry.

Now the mother resorted to reasoning. "You must sit down because the stewardess will be very upset with us, and we are about to take off, and you could hurt yourself." When reasoning did not work, she tried crass bribery: "If you sit down, I will read you your favorite story, and I have a lollipop in my purse." When the child did not rise to the bribe, her mother took the punishment approach: "If you don't sit down right now, you will be spanked the minute we get off of this plane!" But through all of this the child tenaciously stood her ground. Finally, in desperation, the exhausted mother gave up and said, "All right, if you want to hurt yourself, then go right ahead. Stand on the seat and hurt yourself. But don't come crying to me because you bumped your head."

Finally the stewardess came and put an end to all of our misery by firmly telling the child, "Sit down, now." The child obeyed immediately.

As the plane took off, the mother turned to me in frustration and exhaustion, saying, "Kids sure have a mind of their own, don't they? How do they get to be so demanding?" As we talked, I empathized with her, for what exhausted parent hasn't resorted to such tactics at one time or another? Yet as an outsider, it was quite easy for me to see what she could not see—simply that she had capitulated to her daughter at every turn.

The child's tantrum was nothing more than a power play, a classic challenge of wills. And the mother lost big time. The daughter came up against a set boundary, and that made her furious. She howled, she screamed, *she was angry*. And, from the four-year-old's point of view, the behavior actually worked. She got to stand on the seat and defy her mother! Since throwing a temper tantrum seemed to be such an effective way of getting what she wanted, why shouldn't the child interpret all her desires as inalienable rights? Next time, why not be even more insistent, become angrier, so that she could get her way more quickly? Such cognitive reasoning may not be present in a four-year-old, but there is no question the subconscious message would be there nevertheless.

I couldn't help but ponder what kind of adults our children will become if they are not taught to differentiate between desires and rights. What sort of people will they be when they feel entitled to their rage just because they don't get what they want? Seneca, the Roman playwright and essayist, wrote insightfully on the problem of anger. He believed that proper child-rearing is one of the surest methods of immunizing against anger in adulthood. He said that the child "should gain no request by anger; when he is quiet let him be offered what was refused when he wept." *(Moral Essays)*

As we stepped off the plane and walked into the airport, I realized instantly that something was very wrong. It took me a second to figure it out, but there was an eerie silence in the airport, and no one was speaking. Then I saw people crowding around the television monitors. Someone had just bombed the federal building in Oklahoma City. We watched in horror as workers carried out the limp bodies of babies and children. We saw adults staggering from the collapsed building. The news commentators were guessing it was a terrorist attack, no doubt perpetrated on unsuspecting Americans by a group of international terrorists from the Middle East. Little did any of us dream that a few days later the police would accuse two *American* men. It is difficult to imagine men whose anger against the federal system was so intense that they felt they had every right to blow up a large building and murder innocent people in protest.

That catastrophe vividly illustrated what horrible things unchecked and indulged anger can accomplish. The human carnage of the bombing was the result of people believing they were entitled to their rage. The Greek biographer Plutarch wrote words tragically accurate for that moment in Oklahoma City: "We, who tame beasts and make them gentle . . . under the impulse of rage cast off children, friends and companions and let loose our wrath, like some wild beast, on servant and fellow citizens." *(On the Control of Anger)* Suddenly the connection between the child throwing a tantrum on the airplane and the enraged terrorists bombing a building seemed too close for comfort. I was so shaken at seeing the fruit of uncontrolled rage, I determined at that moment to discuss with my children the deadly consequences of refusing to control the impulse to anger.

A few days later I took my kids to a lovely restaurant, and just after we had ordered our food, we heard a lot of commotion. The restaurant was designed so that diners could see into the kitchen. To my astonishment, and to my children's great delight, the cook jumped over the counter and began to slug one of the waiters, who responded in kind. At first my children thought it was part of the evening's entertainment, and they moved their seats for a better view. But after watching the men exchange several blows, everyone realized this was a genuine fight. My son and daughter became frightened. The manager broke up the fight, but what transformed my children's fear into incredulity and then finally to laughter was hearing these grown-up men saying, "He started it!" "Yeah, but you called me a name!" "Oh yeah? Well, you pushed me." My children rolled their eyes and said, "Mom, that's the kind of thing *we* say when we're mad. How old are these guys anyway?"

THE FIRE WITHIN

That was exactly the point. Our uncontrolled anger reveals our childish immaturity to such an extent that even children can label it accurately. Little did I expect that my admonition to the kids on anger would be preceded by such a visual aid! But the point could not have been made more clearly. Children who do not learn to differentiate between desires and rights become adults who are capable of enormous damage in their anger.

Of all the emotions, anger is one of the most common and most powerful. It's considered one of the so-called deadly sins, and for a very good reason: anger can be murderous. Therapists tell us that they spend more time helping clients deal with their anger than with any other emotion. Every day in the news we learn of violence unleashed by anger—rape, child abuse, murder, and gang warfare. In our high schools in this country, it has been reported that two thousand students are physically attacked every hour. There are high schools in Chicago, where we live, that have security systems as sophisticated as those in airports. Students must pass through them before they can enter school; all have to be checked to see if they are carrying weapons.

In his book *The Seven Deadly Sins,* Henry Fairlie says we live in an age of wrath. "There are angry people who seem simply to be angry within themselves, at anything and everything; angry at life, angry at their lot, angry at the world, angry at everyone else, and angry at themselves." At times this wrath seems ever-present in our modern society; it is seen in the terrorist, the murderer, the spouse and child abuser, the kidnapper, the looter, the demonstrator. What is the justification for all the anger? Most would answer simply, *Because I am angry!* In our age, apparently that is reason enough. If people think their anger is justified and that their cause is right, action that leads to destruction seems legitimate. Fairlie writes, "We have come close to the point of giving to Wrath an incontestable license to terrorize our societies."

Why are we so angry? The answer is complex and beyond the scope of this book to analyze comprehensively. But surely one factor in the contemporary epidemic of anger is that we are brought up believing that we are *entitled*. The message of entitlement is omnipresent. Even television commercials aired during children's programming tells them they have a *right* to Sprite!

How is our anger or antagonism aroused? When we suffer a real or perceived injury, we become angry. Fairlie calls anger a "disorderly outburst of emotion connected with the inordinate desire for revenge." Simply put, the angry person wants to punish the perceived offender.

The image often associated with anger is fire. We are not cool-headed when we are angry; instead, we are "boiling mad," as the expression goes. In *The Seven Deadly Sins,* Fairlie associates anger with the "Devil's furnace." In Psalm 39, David expressed his own anger by saying "my heart grew hot within me, and as I meditated, the fire burned." The physical image of that blazing Oklahoma City federal building no doubt corresponded to the inner fire of anger that burned and consumed those who bombed it.

The problem with anger is that it works against its own self-interest. Carriers of anger set their jaws to punish, and in the moment of their unthinking fury, their eyes blaze, voices rise, the fingers point, and the feet stamp. Later the angry person may be horrified over the debris his or her anger has left behind. But in the heat of anger, rational thinking does not prevail. The other problem with anger is that it eventually takes on a life of its own. It can become an addiction that consumes us. It fixates, devours, burns, and lays waste. It harms its carrier and destroys anyone getting in the way. The fire of anger may smolder unnoticed for a long time, but ultimately rage burns its way through people and affects every dimension of their being. The carnage it leaves is unmistakable.

Is all anger bad? Can it ever be justified, and if so, how can we know when it is? Are there proper ways to express anger? What is available to help us cope with our own anger or that of another person? Our next episode with David deals with these kinds of questions and illustrates the potential deadliness of anger. However, for the first time in the biblical narrative, David exhibits not a virtue but a vice!

THE ROAD TO REVENGE: DAVID AND NABAL (1 SAMUEL 25)

Anger is always provoked by something, whether the provocation is real or only imagined in the mind of the one offended. In David's case, it was real.

After Samuel the prophet died and the last bit of moral restraint in Saul seemed to disappear, David and his men moved out of Judah to the desert, where there was less likelihood of being attacked either by the Philistines or Amalekites. However, the sheep farmers of those sparsely populated border areas needed protection for their large flocks from thieves and raiders. David and his men found themselves near the property of a very wealthy man, Nabal, who had thousands of goats and sheep. David decided to provide protection for Nabal's flocks.

What was Nabal like? The text tells us that he was surly and mean in his dealings. Recently I saw a message printed on a shirt that perfectly stated the essence of Nabal's philosophy: The front of the shirt said, "He who dies with the most toys wins." That is why the narrator of Samuel first describes Nabal by his possessions. Nabal's life was determined by his property, and he lived to defend it. The back of the shirt I saw read, "But he still dies nonetheless." If Nabal had been wise, his life-philosophy would have read like this instead.

However, Nabal was not wise. In fact, after Nabal's riches are described, we are told that his name means "Fool." Now, it is unlikely that any mother, no matter how arduous her experience in childbirth, would actually name her son a fool. "Nabal" was probably a popular distortion of his real name, a distortion that suited him perfectly. In any case, he later refused to help David in any way when David and his men were in need.

In his every word and action we see a man who thought of himself as autonomous, subject to no one. He treated everyone around him as peasants to be endured, while he thought of himself as being on the level of a king. It is clear that neither his wife nor his servants respected him, for he was arrogant, self-centered, and mean. Even a servant described him as "a wicked man that no one can talk to." All he had was the power that money could buy.

It is obvious that the narrator of the story wants his readers to remember another foolish king who used the power of his office but did not have any strength of character to inspire those around him. In *David's Rise and Saul's Demise,* Robert Gordon likens Nabal to a diminutive Saul. Indeed, in this section of our text, Nabal acts as Saul's surrogate, for his attitude towards David is exactly like Saul's

Still, Nabal was important to David because his men were in need of a good square meal. Their hopes were slim enough of finding much food in the wilderness, unless of course a farmer of substance could be persuaded to share with them some of his produce. In a conventional Middle Eastern introduction, David sent ten young men to Nabal at shearing time—always a time of lavish celebration and hospitality— to convey David's cordial greeting, but also to deliver the underlying message that there was an obligation to meet. In effect, David told Nabal, "You owe me!" The men explained that David had protected Nabal's men and sheep, implying they could have easily helped themselves to the animals they needed for food. In light of the fact that many of David's men were malcontents, some with backgrounds in crime, it may have been no small thing for a fugitive future king to have controlled them. Yet he did not allow them to mistreat Nabal's shepherds, or to take what did not belong to them even though they were very hungry.

But Nabal had no intention of helping David. While Nabal was technically without obligation to David and his men (Nabal had not requested their help), he should have given them more serious consideration instead of foolishly dismissing them. His very choice of words revealed his pride and self-centeredness. "Why should I take my bread and water, and the meat I have slaughtered for my shearers, and give it to men coming from who knows where?" In other words, Nabal considered David a nobody. "Who is this David? Who is this son of Jesse? Many servants are breaking away from their masters these days." To justify his own greed, he labeled David as a vagrant who had run away from his master, a scathing insult.

David hit the roof when he heard this artless put-down. His response was immediate and harsh. "Put on your swords!" At this point David had six hundred men, and he ordered about four hundred of them to go with him to attack Nabal and show the ingrate who David *really* was. This hasty action on David's part is especially surprising considering the iron self-control he had demonstrated in regard to Saul's truly dangerous threats. Yes, Nabal sorely provoked him, but on the other hand, David had suffered far worse treatment from King Saul. David succumbed to angry revenge, his hot-blooded nature unrestrained for the moment, intent on destroying all the males belonging to Nabal by daybreak.

Not long before, David had told Saul that it was beneath the king to go chasing after him, since Saul was the Lord's anointed. Yet David, who was also the Lord's chosen, sought revenge on this surly sheep farmer. It was not only beneath David to behave like this, but it revealed a temporary lack of trust in God. Whereas David was content to leave the judgment between himself and Saul to God, he now wanted to be judge and executioner of Nabal. Ungoverned anger makes us behave in foolish ways. And if we allow it to control us, we end up looking as foolish and acting as dangerously as the fools who provoke us.

Through David we see that the sin of anger has potentially disastrous consequences. Enraged people in the moment of red-hot indignation are self-righteous and unreasonable. In fact, David displayed an astonishing and unusual lack of good judgment. It is reasonable to assume, as many commentators point out, that Saul spread rumors blaming David for the massacre of the priests at Nob. And with rumors like that floating around, the last thing David needed was a bloody massacre that truly *was* his fault. Furthermore, for David to have killed Nabal and all of his men would be a very dark mark on his future monarchy, for everyone in the kingdom would know about it. But David was in no reasonable frame of mind. He was not thinking about long-term consequences. He only wanted revenge—and he wanted it *now!*

WRONG ANGER VS. RIGHT ANGER

At this point in David's career, he is a virtual object lesson on the wrong kind of anger. However, just as we saw earlier that not all fear is wrong, it is also true that not all anger is wrong. We *should* be outraged in the presence of evil. Not to be angry about child or spouse abuse, or drug-related crime, or the bombing of innocent people in a federal building in Oklahoma City, would itself be wrong. Also, we should not confuse sinful anger with the emotion of anger. David's angry reaction at having been insulted was a normal human response. But he crossed the line into sin when four things occurred.

1) When It Is Wrongly Motivated

David's anger did not stem from righteous indignation, but because his pride had been pricked! Nabal went beyond personally insulting David; he humiliated him in front of his men. The future king was in dire need, yet he didn't come to Nabal with a tin cup in his hand. He came as a peer, as a leader who needed help. But Nabal dismissed him as a nobody. Some powerful and vengeful pride coursed through David's veins as he shouted, "Put on your swords!" One could imagine that his men were thrilled—here at last was some behavior they understood! No more of this bizarre restraint that would not permit them to kill Saul when they had the opportunity. Finally David was seeing things their way!

2) When It Overreacts

David's anger was entirely excessive. How could anyone in his right mind think Nabal's insult gave David and his men permission to massacre all the males in Nabal's household? Preposterous! One of the most dangerous elements of anger is the feeling of being entirely justified in expressing outrageous behavior. When our motives are sinful, we need to cover them with a veneer of self-righteousness. Why? Because we must rationalize our immoral behavior by attributing moral motives to it. As Augustine said, "There never was an angry man who thought his anger unjustified." In such cases, our very vindictiveness and overreaction suggest that our anger is unrighteously motivated. For David, once his motive went awry and his anger was aroused, his response went beyond all reasonable bounds, and it became a sin.

3) When It Intends to Harm

The third element present in sinful anger involves intentional malice. David's anger was not merely an involuntary, momentary feeling. He took deliberate action with the open intent to murder many people. Indeed, David risked the lives of four hundred of his own men for the sole purpose of carrying out his revenge—a highly uncharacteristic response of the usually-cautious David. But in this incident, he allowed anger to reign and lost his capacity for sound judgment. How much better off David would have been to see Nabal's provocation as an opportunity to exercise his will in the practice of self-control, as he had done with Saul.

4) When It Seeks Revenge

Revenge is born of a desperate need to rectify wrongs by inflicting harm on someone in return for a perceived or real injury. The underlying assumption is that God is asleep at the wheel, so it's up to us to help him out of a jam by taking matters into our own hands. Without our personal intervention in correcting this wrong, we fear that injustice will prevail. And that, worst of all, the guilty party will never have to pay the consequences. Revenge is anger at God's seeming powerlessness and a frustration at his slow timing in rectifying wrongs. Novelist Alexander Theroux says that "the sole desire in retribution is to equalize: I'll get even with you." (*Revenge*) This is a great theological blindness, for the avenger is usurping God's job. After all, "Vengeance is mine, saith the Lord."

Yes, there are circumstances when we are to fight against injustice, but not through hatred or the desire to gain a pound of flesh. Not through revenge.

WHAT TO DO ABOUT ANGER

Anger is like any other sin in that it can be more of a problem for one person than another. Few of us, however, are completely free of its grip. Yet anger *is* under our power to control.

Find the Reason

The issue with anger is not to repress it or to let it explode, but, as the Jewish Scripture translates, "Find the *reason* for the source of your anger and sin." That means we need to examine our motives. And once having found the reason or motive for anger, then we must learn to release it in a healthy way. We can't release it unless we are willing to look at its source.

There are many reasons why we get angry and overreact. Sometimes our anger derives from fear and the feeling that we are being threatened. That may in part explain why David overreacted to Nabal. There is no question that he was under enormous pressure. Consider the awesome responsibility of caring for six hundred men holed up for weeks in the desert of Paran. David took a risk moving them into the more inhabited country near Paran, but it was sheep-shearing time and he probably thought it would be easier to obtain food. When his plan backfired, he was desperate, and no doubt felt somewhat powerless. David's feeling of powerlessness may have led to fear and finally to rage because he could not see a way out of this terrible situation.

Sometimes unconfessed sin is the problem. We need to ask ourselves if we are out of control because of something we have been guilty of. It is amazing to see a person scream and point a finger at someone else, when, if the truth be known, it is her own unconfessed sin that is really haunting her.

Sometimes our anger stems from past wounds that cause us to project old debts onto new people. I know a man who carried his father's grief for years. When he was a child, his father had been rudely and unjustly dismissed from his job. The father himself probably stewed for a little while, but then he got on with his life. But not the son. The son was very sensitive and considered what was done to have been a grave injustice. He allowed his anger toward the injustice to fester and grow until it tormented him. Twenty years later this adult son walked into his father's old place of employment and railed at an astonished receptionist for their past mistreatment of his father. The woman no doubt was in diapers when the incident occurred! But this is an example of why it is important to identify the underlying cause of our anger.

Know Yourself

Seneca argued that one of the things that dissipates anger is self-knowledge, and I believe that is true. First we must admit to ourselves that we are angry. Admitting any feeling takes a bit of the edge off, enabling us to get the distance we need to evaluate what we are feeling more objectively. There is enough pressure for most of us on any given day to at least push us into frustration. Perhaps anger will follow.

During the writing of this book, I had a chapter due to my publisher one day by noon. I woke up at five in the morning so I could be sure to get it finished and delivered. But after I sent the children off to school, my computer printer started acting up. I decided that I could fix it, which turned out to be an unbelievably serious error in judgment. In the middle of my fix-it job, I glanced up at the clock and realized I was due at the children's school in five minutes for our quarterly parent-teacher conference.

As I raced out of the room my printer suddenly starting spitting papers out high into the air a mile a minute. I grabbed enough pages as they flew by to fax to my poor, heroic editor, but after my school consultation, I opened my appointment calendar and realized I had just twenty minutes to get to a dentist appointment. I hurried and made it on time, but all I could think of while I was in the chair was that I'd need a blow torch and a chisel to make my way back into my office again because it would be piled high with the papers spat out by my machine.

By the time I left the dentist's office it was time to pick up the kids, and then to take one to a piano lesson and the other to soccer practice. They begged me all the way home to let them have a friend over. I said it was unreasonable to call a friend at 5:00 P.M.! We were all so tired when we finally got home that I was tempted to eat dinner out, but I decided that what would cheer us up most would be a nice, home-cooked meal. After spending the last of what little energy was left on dinner, I heard the delightful refrain of both my children as they walked into the kitchen: "Oh please, Mother, nothing healthy tonight. We can't stand it." It was one of those days.

Those are the daily frustrations of life, and they can frazzle us. But deeper things make us angry, too. I think unresolved emotional baggage may have been one of the reasons for David's excessive response to Nabal. How was Nabal able to get David's goat when David had been through far worse with King Saul?

It is very likely that David's hypersensitivity to being insulted had an emotional link to the past. The truth is that David was used to being dismissed, overlooked, and forgotten. It did not even occur to his elderly father Jesse to include David after Samuel told him to bring all of his sons with him when he came to sacrifice. David was the last and the least, the eighth son, the runt. As a lad, he spent enormous amounts of time alone watching the sheep. When Goliath was taunting Saul and the Israelites, David's brothers had nothing but put-downs for him when he brought their supplies to the camp. Could such taunts and neglect in his youth have left a scar on his soul? If David had come from a more attentive and loving background, Nabal's dismissing him as a nobody would have been a small setback. "Whatever. It came from a pompous fool; nothing to be taken seriously." But for David, it was a knife thrust into his deepest soul. Anger often has its origin in the past; nevertheless, David's overreaction was wrong.

If only David had asked, What is motivating me to be this angry? Is my response to Nabal's insult a bit overblown? What will be the price to my reputation and the kingdom if I indulge my anger in a massacre? What would God have me do? If David had just stopped to reflect on the implications of his decision, he would have stopped himself before anyone else had to.

Find Constructive Outlets

David's anger in the case we have been considering certainly was unjustified. The problem with anger—justified or not—is that this powerful emotion generates energy. We must find a constructive way to deal with this energy because anger can prod us to destructive acts that are difficult to undo later.

I have been in prayer groups over the years in which we have frequently discussed how to handle our children's anger as well as our own. Once during a meeting it occurred to me that if adults sometimes need to use old delay tactics like "counting to ten," or playing a rigorous game of tennis in order to work off steam, why shouldn't we teach our children the same techniques? Thus, when my children start to get frustrated, I say things like, "It looks to me like you're getting frustrated. Before it builds up and gets out of control and you do things that will make me discipline you, why don't you go outside and play basketball, or take a walk and try to figure out what is making you mad?" Physical activity takes the edge off of the energy of anger, enabling those who are offended to think more clearly as to why they are angry. It does not always work, but it does communicate to them that they can control their anger, and that they can choose to use constructive rather than destructive ways of handling frustration so that it doesn't lead to sin. Whether or not this advice would have helped King David I cannot say. But it might have.

We need to remember that the energy produced by justified anger can be channeled to accomplish many good and wonderful things. In this respect, justified anger acts differently from unjustified anger. Anger that is justified directs itself toward reform rather than revenge.

For example, hundreds of mothers whose children have been killed by drunk drivers used their justified anger to form a group called Mothers Against Drunk Driving, or MADD. This organization has positively affected thousands of drivers and drunk-driving laws.

Temper It

Nothing on earth consumes us so quickly as the passion of resentment. St. Augustine once said, "It is better to deny entrance to just and reasonable anger than to admit it, no matter how small it is. Once let in, it is driven out again only with difficulty." His point was that even when anger is rightfully motivated and morally appropriate, we must be extremely careful to temper it because it is so dangerous and so hard to contain in a righteous way.

Remember the dinner party at which both Jonathan and his father Saul became very angry? Saul, in his sinfully motivated anger, threw his spear at his own son and cursed him. However, Jonathan, whose anger was righteously motivated, left the table rather than allow his anger to spill out in words or deeds he might later regret. He didn't deny or suppress his anger; on the contrary, he felt it quite intensely. But he wisely controlled the expression of it.

If we are tortured by our angry feelings, it would help to talk about them with someone who can be objective and make wise suggestions for dealing with them. Our spiritual counselors should help us probe what is inside us that makes us want to cling to our anger. I have also found that praying David's "angry psalms" is an enormous help. David pulls no punches. If he is outraged, he says so. And he expresses his anger with such startling honesty that it helps me uncover and identify what I am really feeling but have trouble admitting.

Also, when I compare my own emotions with the psalmist's ragings, I often find my own anger ebbing away as I recite his words. For example, I've never been so mad that I wanted my enemies' children to be wandering beggars (Ps. 109:10)! Of course, that's how David's ancient culture viewed their enemies. His attitude would be different, no doubt, if he had been raised after the time of Christ where a more compassionate approach to one's enemies is expected. But the Psalms are helpful precisely because they do not shield us from the truth of our human condition.

Our modern tendency is to jump from pain to praise too quickly. We don't want to acknowledge what we are really feeling. But, like it or not, the psalms are full of anger. There is no attempt to conquer the emotion by being nice. The Psalms show us how it feels to be the victim of someone's anger, the target of a person's hatred. The Psalms don't let *us* off the hook, either, for they also reveal how it feels to be enraged to the point of delivering a curse on someone. Psalm 109 is a good example, where David is driven to cry out against his tormentor, "He loved to pronounce a curse—let it come on him; he found no pleasure in blessing—may it be far from him." (v. 17) The Psalms speak to us of anger, lying, and deceit, and when they do, as C. S. Lewis has written, "No historical readjustment is required. We are in a world we know." *(Reflections on the Psalms)*

Though David's anger had been provoked by Nabal's nastiness, there was nothing in his anger that was godly. It was full of fury, pride, and vengefulness. David even felt that God was as upset about things as he was. He was so sure of this that he in effect said to his men, "May God strike me dead if I don't kill everyone in Nabal's entourage. Nabal is going to be punished because he is wrong and I am right!"

How would you have liked to reason with someone in that frame of mind? David was riding in the company of men before whom he had already been humiliated once that same day. How could anyone have talked him out of his anger? How could anyone have lowered his emotional temperature? Yet that is precisely what Abigail succeeded in doing. We are about to meet an extraordinary woman with enormous skill who teaches us about meekness, anger's counterpart. If David shows us how not to deal with anger, and Nabal shows us how not to treat people, Nabal's wife Abigail is a model of how to do both things right.

QUESTIONS AND REFLECTIONS

1. What makes you angry? Is there a pattern to your anger?

2. Is it difficult for you to acknowledge to yourself that you are angry? If so, why?

3. Why is it important to own our anger?

4. Have you found ways to own and express your anger without harming someone else?

5. How do you handle anger that is directed toward you?

6. How can we know whether our anger is sinful or righteously motivated?

7. What techniques have you used to lower the emotional temperature of anger?

Chapter Ten

Meekness:
The Remedy for Anger

THE GENTLE STRENGTH OF ABIGAIL (1 SAMUEL 25)

What image comes to mind when you hear someone described as meek? Isn't it the picture of a Casper Milquetoast with a dishrag handshake? That is because meekness is often confused with weakness. But to be meek in the biblical sense of the term is to be *anything* but weak. The meaning of meekness is closer to the image of a powerful stallion surging with energy, pulsating with vitality, but *tamed*—a majestic creature that has learned to obey its master's command through a small tug at the reins.

Meekness represents great strength, but it is *harnessed* strength. It is when the capacity to use force is the greatest that the choice not to do so can be the most constructive. Meekness does not seek to harm but to work for peace. Abigail's exercise of meekness in the face of David's vengeful anger not only lowered his emotional temperature, but prevented David from disastrous consequences.

Abigail was Nabal's wife, and in every way her character was a complete contrast to her husband's. She was "an intelligent and beautiful woman." Wise, shrewd, full of common sense, spiritual, clearly respected by others, and articulate—everything her husband wasn't.

One of Nabal's servants went to Abigail distressed over what

Nabal had said to David's messengers. The servant told her, "David sent his messengers from the desert to give our master his greetings, but he hurled insults at them. Yet these men were very good to us. They did not mistreat us, and the whole time we were out in the fields near them nothing was missing. Night and day they were a wall around us all the time we were herding our sheep near them." The servant was remarkably candid about Nabal's shortcomings, and he informed Abigail of her husband's shocking behavior: "Now think it over and see what you can do, because disaster is hanging over our master and his whole household. He is such a wicked man that no one can talk to him."

Abigail wasted no time. She knew she must respond to David's request. She organized a small pack train of donkeys loaded to the ears with two hundred loaves of bread, two skins of wine, five dressed sheep, five seahs of roasted grain, a hundred cakes of raisins, and two hundred cakes of pressed figs—a veritable feast of food for an entire army of six hundred men. She told her servants to go on ahead of her to deliver the provisions, just as Jacob had done earlier in regard to a supposedly angry Esau (Gen. 32:13ff.). Without telling Nabal, Abigail set off to meet David herself.

In a scene somewhat reminiscent of Rebecca meeting Isaac, when Abigail saw David, she slipped down from her donkey and bowed down before him with her face to the ground. Imagine how dumbfounded David must have been! Only seconds before meeting Abigail, he was choking with rage, plotting sudden death for every male in Nabal's household because of Nabal's insult and lack of civility. And then, before his eyes appears a mule-train feast and an astonishingly beautiful "lady of the manor" bowing at his feet. Needless to say, this got David's attention!

THE POWER OF MEEKNESS

Abigail seemed to recognize that what lay behind David's anger was wounded pride. So even though she was a woman of great means who was highly respected, the first thing she did was to bow prostrate before David in obeisance, even referring to him as "my lord" and to herself as his "maid-servant." Then she assumed the blame for her husband's foolishness and begged David to overlook what Nabal had said, for he was a wicked man and a fool. While some may see this as merely calculating behavior motivated by self-interest to protect her husband's holdings, it was not the case.

This was a volatile situation with very high stakes. Abigail managed to stop an army in its tracks, armed only with tact and charm, and with a demonstration of deep humility. If she had been prideful, she might have tried to strike a deal with David on the side: "Look, my husband's an idiot, but he need never know that I slipped you some supplies. After all, I am the lady of the manor of this district!" But there was no pride in Abigail. Instead, she protected David's dignity by scarcely mentioning the provisions he and his men needed so desperately, almost as if she'd cooked up a little basket for afternoon tea. She forewent her privileged status as Nabal's wife and humbled herself completely before David. There is nothing as powerful to bring about a change of heart as the presence of humility and meekness in the face of prideful anger. Nabal's harsh words provoked David's harsh response; Abigail's gentle words turned away his wrath.

"Please let your servant speak to you; hear what your servant has to say . . . as for me, your servant, I did not see the men my master sent. Now since the Lord has kept you, my master, from bloodshed and from avenging yourself with your own hands, as surely as the Lord lives and as you live, may your enemies and all who intend to harm my master be like Nabal. And let this gift, which your servant has brought to my master, be given to the men who follow you. Please forgive your servant's offense, for the Lord will certainly make a lasting dynasty for my master, because he fights the Lord's battles." What a woman and diplomat! Abigail won her case before David said a word. In effect, she told David she was saving him from sin and then advised him that if he put aside his plan to attack Nabal and accepted her gift instead, God would give him a lasting dynasty in Israel. Talk about putting a man in an impossible situation!

This was harnessed strength at its best. It is almost certain that

Abigail spoke to David as no other woman had ever addressed him before. She was submissive, but her speech was a brilliant piece of rhetoric appealing to him on both the intellectual and emotional levels. She was bold yet winsome, wise yet deferential. Above all, she spoke to David in spiritual terms that he understood, terms that went straight to his heart.

Abigail modeled how powerful the results can be when we respond to anger intelligently and spiritually, rather than impulsively as David did. She also reminds us that in a volatile situation we must ask ourselves what sin is being committed and what spiritual virtue might be demonstrated by way of contrast.

Abigail's meekness lowered the emotional intensity of David's anger, enabling him to get needed perspective. Anger is such an intense and deeply felt emotion that the last thing someone who is really angry feels like doing is being fair or objective. Nevertheless, gaining objectivity is vitally important when our emotions are running high.

In the exchange between Abigail and David, we get several ideas for helping an angry person get perspective. These can also be adapted as you learn to control your own anger.

PUTTING ANGER IN PERSPECTIVE

Consider the Source of Insult

Abigail's counsel to David was to consider the *source* of the insult. We should do the same thing. We need to ask ourselves if the person who has hurt us is someone we really admire and respect. It is foolish not to listen to the comments of someone we regard. But we can spend a lot of needless energy feeling wounded when the lashes come from someone we do not respect. Abigail tried to get David to understand that Nabal was not someone to respect, and therefore not someone whose opinion should be taken seriously. "You've heard enough to know what he is like," she said in effect. "He is like his name, a fool. How could you possibly let a man like this get to you? It's unworthy of you to respond in this way."

Consider the Style of Correction

One way of determining whether criticism we receive is in fact godly correction is to examine the motive and the style in which it was communicated. In helping David "see the light," Abigail was humble, meek and wise, and she protected his dignity. Her style of correction was meant to esteem him, whereas Nabal's style was intended to condemn and disgrace him.

There are two distinct ways of seeing a person's faults: conviction and condemnation. God *convicts* of sin, whereas Satan *condemns*. The divine purpose in addressing sin is to call us to repent so that we will become the people he created us to be. God's motive in correcting us is pure love. But Satan's motive in addressing our flaws is pure hate. The demonic intent is to produce despair, self-condemnation, and self-hatred because Satan's goal is to decimate, destroy, and kill.

When we're trying to persuade a person who is sinning to do what is right, our purpose must be like God's. We must never correct in a way that reflects judgmental harshness, leading to the despair and discouragement of condemnation. The motive of the heart must be: "I love you too much to see you do this. I want God's best for you. Please repent before it's too late."

While the motive of correction must always be loving, the styles will vary. Some will correct in a more intense prophetic style that reflects God's righteous indignation, as Samuel did. Others will correct in a meek and quieter spirit, as Abigail did. The key is to discern which power is at work in the correction.

With Abigail, it is not difficult to discern which power was at work. Her words here serve as a good warning to us: Never listen to the enemy's accusations, but always listen to God's correction. But we must be careful. If we are feeling despair and self-hatred at a friend's appropriate correction, it may well be that we are filtering those godly words meant to rescue us through the condemnation of the enemy. Remember, when Satan accuses, he uses half-truths designed to hook us into listening. But once we're hooked, his plan is to lead us down the path to despair, bad decisions, and ultimately spiritual defeat. On the other hand, godly correction sees our flaws in the context of our worth. The goal is that we may be all God intends for us to be.

When God corrects us, he convicts us in a way that helps us heal and grow. Abigail modeled this, for what she said and how she said it produced hope in David. He rightly recognized that Abigail's correction was God's conviction speaking through her, and this encouraged him so much that he was able to say, "Praise be to the Lord, the God of Israel, who has sent you today to meet me. May you be blessed for your good judgment and for keeping me from bloodshed."

Consider the Strength of Your Advocate

There is nothing quite so painful as being demeaned—especially to your friends. But Abigail reminded David that his reputation was in God's hands. At the right time, God would promote David, she said. She warned him not to try to settle the score on his own, for that would be reckless and ineffective. "When the Lord has done for my master every good thing he promised concerning him and has appointed him leader over Israel, my master will not have on his conscience the staggering burden of needless bloodshed or of having avenged himself." No, David had to learn to let God be his advocate. And so must we.

There is so little we can do to persuade someone that we are trustworthy once they begin to doubt us. But we should be content to let God have the responsibility to convince others of our character. That is his job, not ours. Like David, we need to develop patience. But we must also learn not to let another person's sin (gossip or slander) provoke us to sin.

There is another option open to us when we have been maligned. It is to leap to our own defense and prove that the one condemning us is wrong. This represents the road more traveled, but it is not an acceptable one. In his spiritual autobiography, the African Bishop Augustine prayed, "O Lord, deliver me from this lust of always vindicating myself." (Confessions) Oswald Chambers took a similar position: "Our Lord never explained anything; He left mistakes to correct themselves." *(My Utmost for His Highest)* Chambers believed that what distracts us from our calling is the thinking that we must try to correct people's impression of us.

Indeed, one of the enemy's devices is to sidetrack us from what we are called to do. And one of the best ways to accomplish this is to tempt us to become involved in minor skirmishes over our reputation. Abigail's counsel to David was to forgo defending himself and to get on with his calling—in other words, to let Yahweh fight his battles.

Consider the Shape of Your Future

In the heat of anger David forgot his bright future. His anger led him to short-term thinking, whereas Abigail wanted him to consider the "big picture." Wise Abigail, who seemed to understand everything, told David that his would be a "lasting dynasty" and that he would be "bound securely in the bundle of the living by the Lord." Actually, these are very pivotal statements in the entire narrative of David's rise to power, for they imply not only that he would be king but that his kingship would lead to a dynastic throne. Abigail implored David to think about his future, and not to behave in a manner that would jeopardize it for him or for the nation.

What was true for David is true for us: if our lives are devoted to the Lord, our futures are every bit as certain as was David's and his dynasty. We are absolutely promised a destiny of hope and not despair. Therefore, we must evaluate every action in the light of eternity. Abigail's counsel to David is also wonderful counsel for us. When we are angry or in despair, and tempted to take matters into our own hands, we should get hold of the big picture of what God wants to do in our lives: Is what we are considering doing worthy of someone with as glorious a future as ours?

THE DECISIVE MOMENT

Would David listen? He was a headstrong and passionate man, and at this point he would have been *especially* sensitive about what he did in front of his men. Nevertheless, his response to Abigail is remarkable. Think of it. David had rallied nearly four hundred of his men to attack

Nabal. He had a lot riding on this decision. Yet when Abigail said her piece—in full view of all of the men and in a culture that had little regard for the opinions of women—David didn't try to save face. He *could* have tried to cover his miscalculation and said, "Listen, men, there's been a *slight* change of plans. This woman realizes that I am totally in the right and that her husband is a worthless jerk. She's just *begging* me to reconsider. So I've decided to do the little lady a favor. After all, you know women. She'll just cry if we turn her away. And anyway, it's nearly noon, and my blood sugar level always drops about now. I need to eat."

No, David admitted (again in front of his men) that he was wrong to be on this particular private crusade and that Abigail was quite right to have kept him from harming innocent people. His actual response was, "Praise be to the Lord, the God of Israel, who has sent you today to meet me." He readily recognized Abigail's wisdom and saw that God was intervening through her. "Then David accepted from her hand what she had brought him and said, 'Go home in peace. I have heard your words and granted your request.'" Only a very strong man could have done that.

It is David's attitude about his error in judgment that is so refreshing. He admitted his mistake openly and freely, as a true leader must. He made no attempt to hide or cover his backside before his men. There was no sense of: "Oh boy, this is very embarrassing. And to be corrected by a woman—oh vey!" Instead, his attitude was worthy of a great leader: "Do you know how lucky I am? I'd already made one mistake, and I was just about to make a much more serious one—and then Yahweh protected me! He intervened before I *really* blew it! Isn't Yahweh great? Don't you see how much he cares? Aren't we blessed to know him?"

This too was an example of meekness. David chose to harness his strength in humility. He chose *not* to use his weapons when he could have. For a moment, this future king of Israel looked like a wild stallion on the loose. But he was a tamed stallion who knew his master's voice, and he also knew that it was his master's hand tugging on the reins. And so David stopped in his tracks and reversed directions toward God's will.

Out of David's mistakes and failures come valuable spiritual lessons for us.

A TEACHABLE SPIRIT

David knew that he was sinful. But out of this experience he realized afresh that God was not only merciful and loving, but he was one on whom David could count to help him to see the errors of his ways and prevent him from greater harm. God did not require perfection of David; nor does he require it of us. What God does require is a teachable spirit that is quick to admit shortcomings and learn from them.

The important thing was how David dealt with his problem once it was identified. He responded to correction with delight and gratitude because he knew that the conviction came from God's loving mercy. God's correction led him to worship.

HOLINESS TAKES PRACTICE

David had shown remarkable self-control with Saul, yet he blew it with Nabal. It is not uncommon to conquer a large problem, only to get sideswiped by a lesser problem when we are not looking. David was caught off guard because he wasn't expecting a sheep rancher to behave as disdainfully as King Saul. David's experience shows us that we must not be discouraged when we fail. Godliness takes practice and perseverance; it is not obtained in a weekend.

LET GOD BRING JUSTICE

The virtue God developed in David was the ability to refrain from treating his enemies as they treated him. God wanted his man to learn that it's not just the "anointed enemy" that David must refuse to strike, but, without God's clear guidance, it is everyone else as well. David learned that he must not be his own agent of revenge, but he must entrust his cause to Yahweh. In the end he saw not only how reckless his anger had been, but how serious the damage would have been to himself and his legacy had he sought vengeance. With David, we must affirm that vengeance belongs to the Lord, not to us. God will bring justice and judgment, and this is very sure, for he is a God who rewards good and punishes evil. And it didn't take long for David to see this truth realized.

Nabal was holding a banquet when Abigail met with David. The host was in high spirits and very drunk, so she decided to wait till morning to tell him what she had done. The next day when the hungover Nabal heard his wife's story and realized what had almost happened to him, "his heart failed him, and he became like a stone." He died about ten days later. Whatever the immediate cause of Nabal's death, the narrator of Samuel wants us to be clear about one thing: God smote him. What David refrained from doing under the direction of Yahweh, Yahweh did himself. The lesson is unmistakable. If vengeance is required, God will act on our behalf.

The conclusion of the Abigail story? After Nabal died, David successfully wooed her as his wife. She was the perfect partner for this headstrong man, for she was intellectually discerning, politically efficient, theologically astute, and her nature was deeply spiritual.

DAVID SPARES SAUL'S LIFE AGAIN (1 SAMUEL 26)

Having learned to wait on God rather than to seek personal revenge, David found himself immediately tested in this area. It is not surprising that the next episode in our story brings him another chance to kill Saul. A piece of intelligence had come to the king from the Ziphites again. Off Saul went to find David, this time to the hill of Hakilah south of Jeshimon. David sent out scouts to locate Saul's encampment. Then he led a group of his men there at night and asked two of his elite soldiers to follow him into the camp. Abishai volunteered. That night the Lord caused a deep sleep to come over Saul and his men. When David discovered Saul asleep, Abishai asked permission to kill Saul with the king's own spear.

But David had learned his lesson well. He replied, "Don't destroy him! Who can lay a hand on the Lord's anointed and be guiltless?"

Instead, David had Abishai retrieve the spear and water jug that were near Saul's head. The spear had come to symbolize so much for Saul—his pathetic attempt at control, prestige, and authority. Taking it was a daring move, for David and Abishai now had proof that they could easily have killed Saul.

When the two men had crossed over the valley and returned to a safe distance, David called out to Abner, the commander of Saul's army and Saul's guard, "Why didn't you guard your lord the king? Someone came to destroy your lord the king. . . . Look around you. Where are the king's spear and water jug that were near his head?"

Saul awoke and heard all of this. He asked, "Is that your voice, David, my son?" At this point David made a spirited defense of his innocence, much as he had done earlier in En Gedi. He asked Saul why he kept pursuing him, what he had done this time.

Saul's response was remorseful. He confessed his sin against David and for the first time took responsibility for his actions. He promised David that he meant no harm and conceded that he had acted foolishly. Never before had Saul been quite so explicit about his wrongdoing. Perhaps this time his repentance was sincere. Then he did something he had not done before. He asked David to return with him. "Come back, David, my son. Because you considered my life precious today, I will not try to harm you again."

But David declined. He had been burned too many times. Instead, he returned Saul's spear, the death symbol, and declared his righteousness and faithfulness. (David did not return the water jug, the symbol of life.) He said he wanted nothing further from Saul but sought only God. God would deliver David, and David would wait until he did. The return of the king's spear symbolized the doom of Saul's reign. Both David and Saul knew very well the importance of the spear in their relationship.

Then Saul offered a powerful blessing to David, acknowledging that David would indeed be the bearer of God's blessing and deserved what God would give him. It is clear that Saul knew David would be his successor. This was the last time David and Saul exchanged words. They never saw each other again.

SORROW VS. REPENTANCE

From David and Saul's final encounter, we learn a lesson about the difference between sorrow and repentance. Why didn't David return to

Saul? The king sounded sincere and repentant. Wasn't David's refusal a failure to respond in meekness and submission to the king? But David had lived with Saul's behavior and had seen enough of his abuse to know he could never trust the man again. The truth is, Saul had been caught red-handed. What else could he have said? We all feel sorry when we are caught.

How do we tell the difference between sorrow at being caught and genuine repentance? The first thing we must ask ourselves is whether the "sorrow" is part of a pattern. Abuse usually goes in cycles. For a while there is regret, but after a period of remorse, the abuser usually gets worse. That was certainly the pattern with Saul. Secondly, we need to compare words and actions. Saul said some wonderful and apparently sincere things to David to his face, but he said and did horrible things behind David's back.

If Saul was truly repentant, he needed to show that he had changed. He might have said something like: "David, I don't blame you for not trusting me. I have hated you and expressed my rage toward you time and again. I've maligned you, spoken evil about you, tried to destroy you. But now I will go to the people and tell them about my sin against you. And I will show you over a period of a year that my behavior really has changed. I don't expect you to believe a word I am saying to you right now. But watch my behavior, and tell me in a year what you have seen."

For Saul to have the nerve to ask David to return immediately—just because he said the right words and shed a few tears after all that Saul had put David through—is a mockery of genuine repentance. Even if Saul had been truly repentant, a frank acknowledgment of and a sorrow for sin would only have been a first step. The next step would have been a forsaking of the sin completely. That step would only be demonstrated with the test of time.

David's reaction to Saul's request teaches us that there is a big difference between forgiveness and reconciliation. We must always forgive our enemies. That goes without question. In fact, we are to forgive our enemies whether or not they are repentant. However, reconciliation only has meaning when those who have offended have repented.

Beyond this, there must be restoration over time, proving that the old behavior has changed. Reconciliation not rooted in truth is a hoax, amounting to pretending there is peace when there is no peace. Without true repentance from Saul, David would have been reconciling with evil. We wouldn't have the Psalms today, because David would not have lived long enough to have written them.

God put David, the future king, through the paces and tested him. Through it all he learned to restrain his anger. He learned the power of meekness, the mistake of seeking revenge, and the difference between forgiveness and reconciliation. No one would have wanted David to go through such a painful learning process. Yet the lessons he learned bring us hope and wisdom as we learn our own lessons, for he teaches us as pilgrims on the same journey with God.

QUESTIONS AND REFLECTIONS

1. How does Abigail demonstrate the biblical meaning of meekness?

2. When have you seen meekness (harnessed strength) used effectively?

3. What are four things you could do to help you gain perspective when you are angry? How would these help?

4. What does God say to do when you want revenge?

5. What is the difference between forgiveness and reconciliation?

6. In what area of your life do you believe God is asking you to demonstrate meekness? List practical ways you might express this quality.

Chapter Eleven

Despair:
A Turning Point,
or the End of the Line?

P art of the training for those who answer suicide calls is learning how to listen. Once I was invited to speak to a citywide gathering honoring a crisis hot line and the staff that managed it. This was an annual lecture, and many well-known speakers had addressed the same group in previous years on the topic "The Art of Listening." However, I was the first woman ever invited to speak. Because I was the first woman to give this lecture, I sensed a bit of anxiety on the part of the organizers that I do well. In fact, they sent me the previous lectures from the past seven years!

Two things impressed me as I listened to the tapes. First, the art of listening is truly difficult. It requires energy, focused attention, and sensitivity. In each of the seven tapes, the speaker movingly addressed the vital importance of developing listening skills. But what struck me next was what the speakers had overlooked, which I took up in my opening lines: "You can master every listening skill in the book. You can learn how to listen deflectively, empathetically, nondirectively, and lovingly. And yet the people you listen to and counsel could still go straight to hell."

I imagine the members of the committee were by now thinking to themselves, *Oh, what a* great *idea to have a woman speaker. Let's be sure to do it again next year!* Then I made my second point. "Because as important as it is to have good listening skills, the really critical issue of life is, *whom do we listen to*? We can invest enormous energy in developing listening skills, but if we are listening to the wrong person, our lives will end in ruin. Or, what if we listen to the right people but refuse to follow what they say? Is it just possible the reason for the despair you hear so often over the telephone is that those without hope weren't listening to the right person in the first place?"

REFUSING TO LISTEN

Much of human despair is the result of not having listened to God, the true source of wisdom. The Bible tells us that God is not playing a cat and mouse game with his creation. He does not say to us, "I'll bet you can't figure out who I am." Nor does he have a buzzer to beep in delight when we go down the wrong alley, like a mouse in a maze. Quite the contrary. God *wants* us to know him.

The proof? He revealed himself to us, and actually entered into his own creation, through the incarnation of Christ. He also reveals who he is in a general way through the created world in which we live, through other people with whom we associate, and through the human conscience. And he reveals himself specifically through the Bible, God's authoritative and final revelation. We simply are left without the option of saying we *would* have listened if God had only spoken. It is God's nature to speak. The issue is whether we have listened and decided to follow the general and specific revelations of his truth.

Not all feelings of despair are rooted in not listening to God. We must be careful lest we be like Job's friends, looking at the pain or crisis of a person's life and mistakenly concluding it must be the result of sin. That only makes the grieving person's pain all the more unbearable. Feelings of despair, for example, are not uncommon when we suffer great loss—the sort of loss involved in losing a child or a spouse, or when our loved ones suffer devastating illness.

Another kind of despair, however, *is* rooted in long-term patterns of rebellion. This is the despair of people who seem to want the truth about their situation, but do not really hear it when it's offered.

Therapists and clergy often say there comes a moment in counseling when it is necessary to speak strong, painful, and difficult words of reality. What separates those who truly want to change from those who merely want sympathy is what they do with the truth. Do they take an honest look at themselves and decide to do the difficult work that change requires, or do they walk off in a huff?

Those who walk away often return in time, looking for fresh comfort in yet their latest crisis. But what they are seeking is sympathy and reassurance. "Tell me that everything is going to be okay. Sprinkle some fairy dust; protect me by reversing the consequences of my choices. I won't do the reflective work that is necessary, I won't look deeply and critically at myself, I won't pursue the spiritual disciplines, but please say what you can to make me feel better. Tell me it really doesn't matter that I value my own comfort more than the truth."

To offer sympathy rather than truth at that critical moment is to do a grave disservice to the person you're trying to help. We should never be callous to anyone's suffering, whether the suffering seems to be deserved or not. Nor should we ever withhold love. But the best way to love those suffering from the consequences of sin is to help them face the sin and call them away from it. We must do so lovingly and compassionately, but we must speak the truth at all costs.

I recently heard a clergy counselor say that to offer solace without a serious desire on the counselee's part to face the truth and change means not only that we are enabling them in their deception, but that we actually could be getting in the way of their repentance and recovery. The fact is, we cannot alleviate the consequences of spiritual rebellion, but we can show those in despair that their feelings of hopelessness are ungrounded so long as they squarely face the truth and are willing to repent and change. In this way the pain of despair leads irrevocably to the mercy of God.

So the question we must ask of people in despair is, are they serious about following God? Are they willing to take an honest look at themselves, or will they run from the truth? This is the crossroads of despair, and everyone at some point has to choose his course. This is where we find Saul.

SAUL AT ENDOR (1 SAMUEL 28)

Imagine that Saul has called the suicide hot line and you are there to answer the call. The king's despair is palpable, and it draws your eager sympathy. He says, "I am in great distress and at the gates of ruin. The Philistines are fighting against me, I have no heart for battle anymore, and God has turned away from me. He no longer speaks to me at all." On the surface, what Saul says is certainly true. He gives you the impression that he has done nothing to cause all of this calamity. But as you listen carefully and take his argument apart, you begin to suspect that not everything is as it seems.

Saul said that God had not answered him. But what about the prophet Samuel? It is true that Samuel had died, but the real question was whether or not Saul listened to him when he was alive. Not since the time of Moses had Israel had such a powerful, authoritative, and towering leader as Samuel. But Saul continually disregarded his instructions.

Furthermore, God had given guidance to Saul through the ancient law of Moses. Saul knew these covenant promises—that Israel was never to fear her enemies but rather to trust completely in the Lord. "Moses answered the people, 'Do not be afraid. Stand firm and you will see the deliverance the Lord will bring you today.'" (Ex. 14:13) "Only do not rebel against the Lord. And do not be afraid of the people of the land, because we will swallow them up. Their protection is gone, but the Lord is with us. Do not be afraid of them." (Num. 14:9) "The Lord said to Joshua, 'Do not be afraid of them; I have given them into your hand.'" (Josh. 10:8) But Saul was estranged from God and unable to stand firm. He would not believe the promises that had been given, and therefore he did not obey.

Saul was never left without a word from God. But he would not submit fully to God's revelation, through Scripture or through Samuel, when he had the chance. As a result, despair and fear were his constant companions.

Having tried all the conventional methods of seeking help to no avail, he was as desperate as a man with incurable cancer who has stopped seeing the experts and is now turning to the quacks. Saul said to his attendants, "Find me a woman who is a medium, so I may go and inquire of her." It is a measure of how far the king had departed from his initial allegiance to God that he would seek out a medium. Previously, in obedience to the Law and to Samuel, Saul had banned such activities in Israel. In fact, after our text reports the death of Samuel, we read that "Saul had expelled the mediums and spiritists from the land." But the king felt so frightened and abandoned at this point that he was willing to ignore even his own royal edict. It is bad enough when we hear of an impatient spouse getting fleeced by a medium whom he asks to call up his deceased wife: "Matilda, honey, *where* did you hide the insurance policy?" But Saul's consultation with the witch of Endor was much more serious considering the spiritual and national implications.

Obviously this was a man who believed there was nowhere else to turn. But we must not miss the truth here: that Saul would never have fallen into such hopeless straits and experienced the silence of heaven if he'd listened to God—and God's messengers—all along.

THE RETURN OF SAMUEL (1 SAMUEL 28)

"So Saul disguised himself, putting on other clothes, and at night he and two men went to the woman." What a seedy scene! The king himself crept surreptitiously like a criminal in the night so that he and his men could visit her without being recognized. When Saul asked her to consult a spirit for him, she exclaimed, "Surely you know what Saul has done. He has cut off the mediums and spiritists from the land. Why have you set a trap for my life to bring about my death?"

But Saul assured her of immunity from punishment by swearing, "As surely as the Lord lives, you will not be punished for this." Talk about faint assurance! Think of the incongruity of this, that while in the process of breaking God's law, the king of Israel promised God's protection.

Reluctantly, the woman agreed. She asked, "Whom shall I bring up for you?"

Then the words she could not have imagined were spoken: "Bring up Samuel." *Samuel,* the champion of Jewish orthodoxy! The very man who would most abhor the evil practice of the necromancer, and the man who would have called for the severest treatment possible for practicing mediums. If Samuel was not a man to mess with in this life, what hope would there be that he was any different as a visitor from the world beyond?

"When the woman saw Samuel, she cried out at the top of her voice and said to Saul, 'Why have you deceived me? You are Saul!'" Although we do not know how she recognized Saul, the text implies that she left the room right after Samuel appeared, leaving the pair to themselves. Why?

Well, how would *you* like to explain the practice of a forbidden profession to the towering, thundering prophet Samuel? What would you say? "Oh my, well, isn't *this* an unexpected surprise and honor! I bet you have an objection to what I do for a living. And I'd love to talk with you about it. But why don't we do it the next time you drop by for a visit? For now I'll just leave you two to catch up on old times." Of course, she never had such a conversation with Samuel, but the text does imply that she was out of Saul's sight during the deliverance of the oracle. I don't blame her.

There has been a great deal of debate through the ages about whether this actually was the spirit of Samuel that Saul spoke with. Would a necromancer be an appropriate mediator between the divine and human worlds? Why would God allow Samuel to be brought from the world beyond through a means that the Bible steadfastly condemns? The narrator does not clearly answer these questions, but it is clear that he believes the dialogue between Samuel and Saul reveals divine truth.

It was instantly obvious that death had not mellowed Samuel! His first words were, "Why have you disturbed me by bringing me up?"

Saul said, "I am in great distress. The Philistines are fighting against me, and God has turned away from me. He no longer answers me, either by prophets or by dreams. So I have called on you to tell me what to do."

What Saul really wanted was for Samuel to reassure him that his previous disobedience would not affect his chances of victory, and that the battle would fall to Israel. However, Samuel was still the faithful prophet of the Lord, and he would not reverse what God had already spoken to Saul. "The Lord has done what he predicted through me. The Lord has torn the kingdom out of your hands and given it to one of your neighbors—to David." Furthermore, said Samuel, Saul and his sons would die the very next day, and the Lord would hand the army of Israel over to the Philistines. Saul, a failed, pitiful figure, fell prostrate to the ground, his kingship gone, his power nullified.

Why had the Lord turned from Saul? Samuel's explanation was still the same as when he was alive: "Because you did not obey the Lord or carry out his fierce wrath against the Amalekites." His answer cut to the core of the problem. The root of Saul's despair began long ago, when he stubbornly refused to listen to God.

We may wish that Samuel had spoken to Saul with more compassion. After all, Saul phoned the suicide hot line in despair. But for all Samuel's testiness, let us not forget that he shed many tears over Saul in his earthly life, like a father over a wayward son. Samuel cared deeply for Saul. Even Samuel's prediction of Saul's death was a warning that Saul had only twenty-four hours left to repent and get right with God. Absolutely nothing would ever make this prophet deviate from the Lord's will. He made it clear that Saul's record had not changed, and neither had God's verdict.

After Samuel left, the medium saw the pathetic sight that was Saul in a heap on her floor. She knew that he needed help. Indeed, he had not eaten all day and night. So the medium twice reminded Saul that she had "listened" (or "hearkened" and "obeyedst," as the *Revised Standard* and King James versions put it) to him at great risk. Now, she insisted, it was Saul's turn to listen to her and accept her food so that he could regain his strength. At first Saul would neither listen nor eat, but eventually his men joined the woman and persuaded him, and they ate.

Saul had begun well, yet from the beginning he stubbornly resisted obeying the voice of the Lord. When we think of his promising start and then the contemptible ending to his career, we can only regard his story as tragic. When Saul was first introduced to the reader, he was seeking help from Samuel because he knew that Samuel was "a man of God . . . highly respected." (1 Sam. 9:6) But by the end of his reign, Saul was seeking help from a medium. At the first meal where we observed Saul eating, Samuel had placed him at the honored end of the table in recognition that he would become king. The prophet said emphatically, "Eat, because it was set aside for you for this occasion. . . . " (1 Sam. 9:24) But the last meal Saul ate was prepared by a witch, who also gave him an emphatic order to eat. That first meal was given as a covenant with God, but Saul's last meal was a covenant with evil. The contrast could not be more stark.

Saul's tragedy could have been averted if he had only listened to the right person. But he could never make up his mind whom to listen to. He listened to his soldiers when they pressured him to take the Amalekite booty. He listened to a medium who told him to eat, even though it was an act of piety to fast before a battle. But he would not fully heed God's prophet Samuel, and therefore he never listened to Yahweh. Saul's despair was the outcome of his willingness to compromise with evil in order to escape the word of the Lord. It is hard to imagine a more terrible situation in which to find oneself. Saul was not willing to sink his own will wholeheartedly in that of the Lord. He wanted to savor the authority and power that came with the throne, but refused himself to be fully subject to higher authority, God himself.

LESSONS TO LEARN

What can we learn from Saul's despair? There may be many reasons for despair, but there are two causes that I would like to explore. First, our despair may be tied to stubborn disobedience. Second, it may be linked to false faith.

Saying No to God

Our hearts go out to people in despair, but our compassion must be seasoned with discernment. Is despair caused by a stubborn refusal to obey God's clear guidance? Are we seeking guidance about something that has already been revealed? Do we discount God's answer because it is something we do not want to hear?

Saul was told that the kingdom had been given to David, but he would not accept this decision. Even at this late date, he sought the spirit of a dead man who had become his antagonist in life, in the hopes that Samuel would change his mind and give him better news.

As tragic as the king appears, and as much as Saul calls forth our sympathy, we must recognize the stubborn strength of his willfulness. There was something in Saul that would not bend. His refusal to accept defeat, acknowledge his sinfulness, and submit to God is almost unbelievable. But if his life teaches us anything, it is that we must not cling to willfulness against God. If we continue in our rebellion, the only fruit awaiting us is despair and, in the end, destruction. No more dangerous path could we take than opposition to God.

The good news is that God is gracious. He allows us to experience despair so we can get back on track. Think how awful it would be if we were rebellious and perfectly happy. God has made us in his image, so when we violate his ways we do not function properly. Our misery, then, is good news, not bad. When we hit the proverbial wall and feel that life is hopeless, this is the evidence of God's mercy and care, for the Spirit of God is after us, hunting us down, calling us to look straight to him for help, leading us to repent. It may be too late to change the consequences set in motion by our sin, but it is *never* too late to be restored to fellowship with God.

However, Saul never got on his knees and asked God to forgive him for his rebellion. He was disobedient to the end. Israel's first king was a tragic figure because he would not listen to and obey God, even in his despair. For all time Saul stands as a symbol of the futility of rebellion.

Saying No to Authentic Faith

Saul's despair also stemmed from the fact that he certainly did not have a heart knowledge of God. He had a faith of sorts—a nervous desire to "get it right" when it came to external religious details—but it amounted to a strange duty to the externals without a genuine devotion to God. For example, the king strongly resisted taking the meal from the medium because he was fasting. If his fast was due to the prescribed battle ritual, which it almost certainly was, it meant he was fasting out of religious obligation on the way to see a witch! That is like tithing on the way to see a prostitute. Saul never appeared to be a man whose heart had been strangely warmed by God, as John Wesley described his own conversion experience. There was a kind of superstitious feeling to his faith, a false piety, a form of legalism.

Is our own despair the result of having played at religion without having a deep love for God? The problem with legalism is that it trivializes God. To appease God by obeying external rules does not really take him seriously. Nor does it speak highly of God's basic intelligence. What kind of creator could be so easily duped by such behavioral tricks? One senses that Saul engaged in religious duties as a means to hedge his bets in order to get God's favor. That is not true faith.

I know a couple who have a bright and vital faith in God today, but they have had to overcome elements of legalism from their background. She once told me, "When I was growing up, it was always very clear how to tell who was not a Christian. A Christian would *never* swim on Sunday." Her husband protested with a twinkle in his eye, "Oh, that's ridiculous. Christians could *swim* on Sunday. They just couldn't *dive*!"

God cannot be controlled by fasting or tithing or church attendance, or by anything else. False faith looks at life and says, "Let's see, can I get away with this—bend the rule here, sneak around the obvious rule there—and still get to heaven?"

Saul seemed to play that kind of religious cat and mouse game, following the formal rules so as to get what he wanted. But his relationship to God was never heartfelt.

The vital lesson of Saul is that we must sink our own will into the Lord's and establish an intimate relationship with him. Saul always refused to do either, choosing instead to try to appease the Lord through external obedience, asserting himself rather than accepting the will of God. The fruit of Saul's false faith was despair. It is the inevitable destination for those who refuse to listen to God.

WHAT TO DO ABOUT DESPAIR

There are many reasons for despair. It may come from finally facing the consequences of sin. Or it can come from just the opposite—from *refusing* to face our sin. Most of us experience some despair when we suffer a traumatic loss. It is important to discern the reason for the despair if we would help those in the grips of this emotion.

When Despair Comes from Sin

One of the most difficult tasks in caring for people in despair is discerning if their problem comes from something they did wrong and won't admit. Saul is a good example of this type of despair. He wallowed in self-pity and blamed everyone but the true culprit—himself.

What makes matters worse is that people whose despair is sin-rooted are often highly manipulative, and they know exactly where to go for sympathy. They usually choose sensitive, loving people who lack discernment. These caregivers want to relieve everyone's pain, but they don't feel comfortable asking the tough questions. However, to offer sympathy without understanding the truth of the situation does a grave disservice to the person you are trying to help.

So what can caregivers do? First, they must not succumb to a sentimental love that regards empathy as the only virtue in love. They must ask themselves tough questions: Why did this person choose to talk with me? Whom else has he or she spoken to? If I discover she has lied to me, am I objective enough to confront her with the truth, or will I cover it up with empathy? Do I see any genuine ownership of faults? Caregivers need to weigh the responses they get to pointed questions such as: "You tell me you had a skirmish with the law (or an adulterous affair) when you were young. Has that ever been repeated again? If so, when? Have you confessed that sin to the appropriate person?" We cannot help people unless we know they are speaking the truth. That does not mean we are not caring or loving. On the contrary, it is love that demands the truth.

Sometimes people in despair have confronted their sin, but they can't see any reason for hope. It may be too late to reverse the consequences of their choices, but it is never too late to hear why we have reason to hope. According to reliable accounts, the serial killer Ted Bundy turned in his despair to God and became a Christian. His life at the end was dramatically changed by his confession of sin. He could not bring the people he had murdered back to life, any more than he could have changed his own sentence of death. He paid for his crimes in the electric chair, but he used his last days to speak about the consequences of sin and to call others to Christ.

Give God a Chance

There is another reason for despair that was not a part of Saul's experience, but that is oftentimes a direct cause of our grief—trauma. In those times we need to cling to God more than ever, but so often our hope has been wounded. When that happens, very often God gives us other faithful people from whom we can draw strength.

As a college student, I went to L'Abri (French for "shelter") in Switzerland. It is a study center and community begun by the late Francis A. Schaeffer for students from all over the world and from all walks of life who are searching for truth and reality. Many were there wishing to integrate their faith with the academic disciplines. I had read Schaeffer's books, and I was curious as to what sort of person he would be. I hadn't been there a week when I found out.

My new roommate told me that she had been sexually abused by her father and brothers, diagnosed an alcoholic at sixteen, and had been continually involved in the use of drugs. The message she had heard all of her life was that she was trash. When you hear that long enough, you believe it. And what do you do with trash? You dispose of it. That was what she was trying to do with her own life—dispose of herself in one way or another.

One night she came in drunk, and another night she was high on drugs. By the third or fourth night she had taken some lethal combination of pills, and she had to be rushed to some medical emergency center.

Dr. Schaeffer had been out of the country lecturing. He returned that night, exhausted after a long trip. But when he discovered what serious trouble this newcomer was in, he immediately went to her and stayed by her side for many hours that night. When she finally returned to our room the next day, the look on her face was almost impossible to describe. She looked at me with eyes as wide as saucers, and she said, "Becky, he didn't get mad at me for breaking all the rules here. He held my hand. And he begged me to give God a chance. He had tears in his eyes when he heard all the junk that had happened to me. He cared so much for my pain. But he told me over and over, 'Please, just give God a chance. He loves you. He can help you. Don't lose hope.' I told him, 'I have no hope. It's been beaten out of me.' And he said, 'I understand. Then hang on to my hope. Lean on *my faith* till you have your own. Trust my hope for what God can do in your life. Just please give God a chance.'"

That woman stayed at L'Abri for a long time, and as she was slowly nursed back to physical and emotional health, her life was completely transformed. Her despair turned to hope not because she had the inner resources of her own at first, but because she was willing to open herself to God in whatever way she could. She was able to give God a chance by leaning on someone else. Then one day her hope in Christ was truly her own.

QUESTIONS AND REFLECTIONS

1. What has caused you to feel despair?

2. What would you say to a person in despair about why there is a reason to have hope? What shouldn't you say?

3. Describe the kind of person who has helped you in your despair, and then describe the kind of person who has hurt you.

4. The author distinguishes the despair that is caused by rebellion from the despair caused by profound suffering. How can you determine the root of a person's despair?

5. What has been the value of suffering in your life?

Chapter Twelve

Hope:
The Remedy for Despair

G K. Chesterton said that "hope means expectancy when things are otherwise hopeless." But what is hope? Is it closing one's eyes and crossing one's fingers, and then wishing hard for something good to happen? Does that mean that even when there is no rational ground for hope we cling to it nonetheless? Is this what the Bible means by hope?

DAVID HAS THE ANSWERS

David and Achish (1 Samuel 27)

When we last saw David, he said to Saul, "May the Lord value my life and deliver me from all trouble." (1 Sam. 26:24) Yet despite all of God's faithfulness and protection, Saul's pursuit had finally rattled David enough to flee Israel. He thought to himself, "One of these days I will be destroyed by the hand of Saul. The best thing I can do is to escape to the Philistines. Then Saul will give up searching for me anywhere in Israel, and I will slip out of his hand." And that is exactly what David and his six hundred men did.

Imagine going to the hated Philistines, Israel's deadly foe, and forging what would appear to be an alliance. Only David would risk doing such a risky and unconventional thing. But then only David could pull it off!

David turned to Achish, the Philistine king, for refuge. We see in this venture what we have always known about David; he could charm the socks off of anybody! As a matter of fact, David was so brilliant, cunning, and charismatic that King Achish not only welcomed him, but at David's request gave him the town of Ziklag for his six hundred men and their families to settle in. This was remarkable not only because David had successfully fought the Philistines in the past, but because the last time David had encountered Achish, he had feigned madness in order to escape without being harmed. David's acting skills seemed only to have improved with age, for he was able to convince Achish that he was on the side of the Philistines.

The Philistine Deception (1 Samuel 27 and 29)

David then played a cunning game of subterfuge. He directed attacks against the plunderers who despoiled Judean as well as Philistine towns. His policy was not only to raid but to exterminate, which was imperative so that informers could not be left to tell tales. What David reported to Achish was that he and his men had actually attacked Judea or her allies. But with no one left to contradict the story, how could Achish be the wiser? "Achish trusted David and said to himself, 'He has become so odious to his people, the Israelites, that he will be my servant forever.'"

We must pause to consider the amazing hold David had over his men. We live in an age of political leaks, where former employees can hardly wait for the ink to dry on their book contracts before they "tell all" about their famous employer. But David's men were completely loyal. It is astonishing that in all the time they spent in Ziklag—a year and four months—none of the six hundred men leaked information about David's misrepresented raid. No one ever released a "David Dearest" exposé.

However, David found himself in a terrible quandary when the Philistines decided to attack Israel. No future king of the nation of Israel could ever fight against his own people. But David could not show any hesitation to the Philistine king either, so he and his men joined the Philistines and marched at the rear with Achish.

They had been in many tight spots before, but even David must have wondered how God would untangle him from this one. When all of Achish's forces had gathered, the other Philistine army generals took one look at David in the rear guard and asked Achish, in essence, "Have you lost your mind? Why are you sending David into battle against his own people? Send him back at once!"

Achish insisted they could trust him, saying, "Is this not David, who was an officer of Saul, king of Israel? He has already been with me for over a year, and from the day he left Saul until now, I have found no fault in him."

Fortunately for David, the Philistine commanders refused to listen. Achish was forced to tell David how desperately sorry he was, but that David and his men would have to return to Ziklag. David feigned astonishment: "But what have I done? What have you found against your servant from the day I came to you until now? Why can't I go and fight against the enemies of my lord the king?"

Achish begged David to understand and to return in peace. He told David that while the commanders did not approve of him, David was "as pleasing in my eyes as an angel of God." In seeming sorrow, David and his men returned to Ziklag.

Imagine the conversation among David's men on the way home to Ziklag: "Was that a close call or what? That Achish, he's a good old sock, but he doesn't know when to come out of the rain! Did you see how downcast he was when the commanders wouldn't let David fight? And David looked *so* heartbroken not to be able to go to battle!" David was their hero, because in this extremely dangerous game with the Philistines he had played and won without ever having worked against the interest of his own Israel.

Although this is the only part of the narrative devoid of the explicit mention of God, there can be no mistake that the Lord had come through for David once again. He had gotten himself into profound difficulty. Yet, God's plan and promise that David would one day be king of Israel was being worked out even through the deception of Achish.

The Amalekites (1 Samuel 30)

The first day's walk back home must have been exhilarating. But the journey back to Ziklag was a long one, for they walked twenty-five miles in three days. By the third day they must have thought continuously about the prospect of home-cooked meals, their wives' joyous greetings, and the routine of kissing and tucking their children into bed. All the comforts of home.

Nothing could have prepared the men for what they saw when they came to Ziklag. Their city was burned to the ground; there was not a person or an animal left on the premises, just a chilling silence. At first the men must have run in horror from home to home, terrified they would see their wives and children slain. Then it sank in: Their families had been captured. On the one hand, this was good news, for no one had been killed. But at that particular point they feared they would never see their loved ones again. David and his men "wept aloud until they had no strength left to weep."

David's loss was as bad as anyone's—both his wives, Ahinoam and Abigail, had been taken. His men quickly turned their frustration, bitterness, and anger on their leader. Why had he left the city undefended?

For the first time ever, David's men spoke of stoning him. When David heard this, "he was greatly distressed."

Never had David been more alone. Saul had long wanted him dead, and now so did his men. He had lost his wives, his land, and all of his possessions, and now his public role as a leader was in jeopardy. But the text says, "David found strength in the Lord his God."

Remember that Saul was also described as "greatly distressed" when he faced his own crisis with the invading Philistines. Saul and David both experienced their lowest moment at the same time! Yet their responses to the crisis could not have been more dramatically different. Saul panicked and sought help from a medium, revealing a man who was both pathological and pathetic. David sought help from the Lord and continued to be faithful and obedient.

Though he seemed to have nothing, David had everything, for he knew whom to turn to in crisis. He did not need any "second-hand" religion; he knew the source of his strength. So David called for the ephod from the son of Ahimelech, the priest. The ephod was an ancient method God allowed for asking for specific guidance. The question the son of Ahimelech asked was: Should David pursue the Amalekites? The Lord assured David that he should, for "you will certainly over-take them and succeed in the rescue." So David rallied his exhausted men and they set out into the wilderness.

Action was probably a good antidote for their frustration. Nevertheless, the traveling proved too much for a third of the men, so David left two hundred of them at the Besor Ravine with the baggage. Imagine the scene. David's army, now two-thirds of its original size, was traveling in the unpopulated desert of the south. They had no idea where the Amalekite raiders were to be found, only that God told them to go.

How did God lead David to the raiders? Through a half-dead Egyptian left lying in the field! He was a slave of the Amalekites who had been abandoned due to illness and left to die. Once his spirit had been revived through food and water, he was able to lead David to the precise spot where the raiders had camped. How like God to answer a desperate prayer using so little, yet with such impeccable timing. And what was required for such provision from the Lord, especially when every circumstance screamed out that God had abandoned them? *Faith* on David's part.

David and his men found the Amalekites "eating and drinking and reveling." David's army wisely waited until dawn when the raiders would be least effective. The triumph over them was massive and com-plete. David fought them "from dusk until the evening of the next day, and none of them got away, except four hundred young men who rode off on camels and fled." Everything was recovered—people and prop-erty, flocks and herds. The same men who had turned against David the day before now believed that he was unquestionably the hero of the hour. David and his entourage returned to Ziklag "having recov-ered everything the Amalekites had taken, including his two wives. Nothing was missing: young or old, boy or girl, plunder or anything else they had taken. David brought everything back."

David and Saul were two men in dismal, terrifying situations. One overcame and conquered; the other sank to despair and ultimate defeat. What enabled David to have hope in such a desperate situation? How was he able to see the village of Ziklag burned to the ground, homes destroyed and abandoned, himself threatened with murder, and *still* have hope? It was all because of God, in whom David's hope rested.

THE ESSENCE OF HOPE

Hope is inseparable from faith in the true God. David is a wonderful example of this. His hope was tied irrevocably to his confidence in God. David knew that God was trustworthy, loving, holy, and just. He knew that God's goodness could never be exhausted. And the fruit of David's hope in God was that it gave him patience to wait and a steadfastness that probably wasn't natural to his temperament. His hope also enabled him to suffer honestly but well.

Too often, though, we twist the truth and begin to think hope rests in ourselves, in a "can-do" approach to circumstances. But we need to be reminded of where our hope lies, because so often we seek it in the wrong places.

Hope Does Not Depend on Present Circumstances

The Lord told Samuel that David would be king over Israel. Jonathan told David that he would be the next king. At long last even King Saul conceded it. Yet there was virtually no circumstantial evidence to convince David that this was to happen. He was driven from the palace due to Saul's murderous envy. He lived like a fugitive for years on end. His life was constantly threatened, his reputation trashed; men continually betrayed him by informing Saul of his whereabouts. Then for a moment it seemed he had lost even his wives and his leadership.

Yet, in each and every experience, David had hope. Why?

Because he did not believe his future depended on the difficulties he faced in his current circumstances. His hope was in God, not in what was happening on a given day.

Hope Does Not Depend on Our Adequacy

When David saw the burned-out village of Ziklag, he wept until he had no more strength to weep. That kind of vulnerability before his men really was amazing. As a leader, he did not hide his grief from his men for fear it would discredit him or discourage them. He did not try to appear in control by suggesting, "I knew this was going to happen. *I told* God I didn't think it was smart to leave Ziklag unprotected." He did not pretend to have God figured out by saying, "Here is what God's teaching us through this." No, David offered no explanation and no cover-up. He wept just as his men wept, in utter distress, standing in absolute solidarity right along with them.

David's ability to be real speaks volumes about his theology. He always knew how dependent and needy he was before a faithful Yahweh. Many Christians get themselves and God mixed up, forgetting who is and who is not in charge. We try to control our own lives, the lives of others, and even God. But the Ziklag experiences of our lives should remind us that God controls all events. David had no illusions about his ability to solve all of life's problems. But he trusted a mighty God who could take a mess and redeem it. David's hope in God was actually strengthened because of his own personal inadequacy.

Our culture puts a lot of pressure on us to be self-reliant and to "believe in ourselves." We are told we can do anything we set our minds to! While such encouragement can motivate us in a positive way, sooner or later will come a Ziklag experience to teach us how woefully inadequate we really are. Our strength and confidence need to rest not in our imagined proud independence, but in God's real power. We are called to "be strong in the grace that is in Christ Jesus" and "strengthened with all power according to his glorious might so that you may have endurance and patience." (2 Tim. 2:1; Col. 1:11)

Hope Does Not Depend on Positive Thinking

We also hear a lot today about the need to practice positive thinking. No matter how bad a situation is, we are told, we must see it as an opportunity. There is a sense in which this is true, because hope does enable us to see reality through a positive lens. But the danger in this point of view comes when we are in such a rush to be positive that we refuse to acknowledge things that are genuinely negative.

Let us not forget that David, who had deep hope in God, took one look at Ziklag and sobbed. Can you imagine his reaction if someone had said, "Now just remember, David, this isn't a problem to solve but an opportunity to conquer!" *That* person would have been sacked on the spot! It was because David's faith was founded in God and not in the strength of his positive personality that he was able to have hope when he needed it most.

Hope is not tied to an upbeat temperament. This is not to say that temperament plays no part. One person may experience joy or peace more easily than another. But hope is a trust, an expectation, and a way of seeing life that is rooted not in our joy or peace but rather in our faith in the true God. When crisis comes, as it always will, the issue is not whether we can remain positive but whether God remains in control. He does! Therefore, we do not have to be self-confident to possess hope. We only need to be God-confident.

Hope Does Not Depend on Having a Blueprint for the Future

God did not tell David how he was going to guide him through the Ziklag crisis. When David asked God if he should pursue the Amalekites in order to rescue the wives and children, the Lord's answer was clear but abbreviated: "Pursue them. You will succeed." So David immediately gathered up his troops and left.

He could have easily resisted and said, "Lord, you are asking me to take six hundred exhausted men, who have already walked a long distance, out into the wilderness? There are no gas stations out there to give us directions. I don't know where I am going, and I haven't the faintest idea where the Amalekites are hiding. Couldn't you just give me a clue as to where you are taking us?"

But God told David no more than that he should go. He wanted David and the men to trust him for each step along the way. But first they had to do what he said. What is required of us in dire circumstances is not our ability to know the future, but our faith in the One who does.

Hope Does Not Depend on the Fairness of Life

David's capacity for hope was strengthened by his realistic understanding of how life works. He did not expect life always to be easy or even fair. I think David saw daily problems as the inevitable hazards of living on planet Earth. But these difficulties were also seen as occasions for God's grace and help. If we likewise accept the fact that life is not always fair and that it can be difficult, this can enable us to live from faithful strength instead of from frightened anxiety.

God prepared David to become a king, not an easy task. All noble things are difficult. God is doing the same work in our lives that he was doing in David's life—bringing us into glory and making us suitable for heaven. He did not shield David from the requirements of becoming spiritually mature, and neither will he shield us.

THE WAY OF HOPE

Since hope is not tied to present circumstances, human resourcefulness, or temperament, what then is it tied to?

Reflecting on the Past

Our hope can be increased when we reflect on what God has done in the past. For example, reflecting on the activities of God and God's people as recorded in Scripture is a great encouragement. When we read of God's faithfulness to Abraham, Joseph, David, or the disciples in the early Christian church, it strengthens our faith and stimulates our hope. We are part of the same assembly of the saints as the people we read about in the Bible, and God will preserve and care for us as he has for his people since the beginning of time. We can read these accounts over and over again to find the strength and hope we need for whatever we are facing in our own lives.

Another way our hope can be increased is to reflect on what God has done in *our* past. I did undergraduate work at the University of Barcelona in Spain. While at the university, I attended an international student conference in Mittersill, Austria, where I heard an Englishman named David Bentley-Taylor preach magnificently on the book of Acts. I developed a warm friendship with David and his late wife that has lasted to this day.

When I returned to Barcelona I had frequent conversations with my roommate, Ruth Siemens, over what career I should pursue when I graduated. Ruth felt strongly that I should work with a collegiate ministry called Inter-Varsity Christian Fellowship. But I resisted because I was sure this would not bode well with my father. My father is a wonderful man, kind and warm, though by his own admission at that time, not a Christian. He is also a very practical and successful businessman. The thought of telling him that I was going into Christian work, with what I knew he would consider a paltry salary—especially after he had sent me to a European university and later to graduate school—gave me reason for pause.

But Ruth never lost hope in what she believed was God's future for me. One day at dinner she said, "Becky, if the Lord wants you to go into Christian work, he will do something beyond your greatest expectations. I have been praying about your father's response. Just wait and see. God will open the door in an unmistakable way!" I just rolled my eyes, thinking she had been in the Spanish sun for too long.

A few days later I received a letter bursting with enthusiasm from my mother, who was already a believer. She said she had attended our home church in Illinois and heard one of the most powerful sermons she could ever remember from a visiting preacher. She wrote, "This man said that what the world needs are committed young people who will carry the Gospel to university students. And, Becky, I immediately thought of you!" And she added, "The man who preached was named David Bentley-Taylor." I was flabbergasted and stunned that God had spoken through someone who was already a close personal friend. If Mom was in my corner about the direction I should take professionally, I knew she would talk to Dad. I think Ruth would have to confess that she gloated a bit as we rejoiced over the letter!

A few years ago I was on a speaking tour in England and I visited the Bentley-Taylors. Out of the blue, David asked, "Becky, how did you happen to go into Christian work?" I could not believe that in all the years of our long friendship I had never told him the story. He was astonished to hear how God had used him, and he asked if I knew more or less the date he had preached at my home church. I did. He went into his library and came out with a personal journal. (He keeps meticulous journals that span decades.) And there he found it, an entry that indicated he had preached at First Presbyterian Church in Champaign, Illinois. His journal noted that he had been impressed by the enormous warmth and response of the members there, one of whom happened to be my mother.

Remembering God's sovereignty and past faithfulness to the church at large and to us personally is a wonderful way to increase our hope for the present.

Seeing God in the Present

We are meant to be encouraged by remembering how God remained faithful in the past, but if our hope is to deepen, we need to recognize God's activity in our lives in the here and now.

The problem with day-to-day living is that we get so obsessed with our own petty concerns that we forget the grandeur of God. That is why worship is so crucial. It brings us back to what matters most. Worship not only gives us a welcome relief from ourselves, it enables us to sense the mystery and glory of God that we so often forget in the busyness of our day. When we worship with others among whom God's Spirit dwells, no matter what kind of week we have had, we can step outside ourselves and focus on being part of the new humanity that God created us to be, unified and holy, and ready to extend the kingdom of God into the world and into our own hearts.

A few weeks ago my children and I were hurrying to get ready for church. Everything that could have gone wrong that morning did in fact go wrong. David was upset because he couldn't find *the* socks he wanted. Elizabeth wanted to wear an outfit I didn't think was appropriate for church. The cereal wasn't right, the microwave was on the blink, and I needed to thaw something fast for Sunday dinner. In short, I was getting crabbier by the minute as I rushed the kids to the car. Shall we say our ride to church was not exactly filled with an atmosphere of wonder and praise? But something happened that Sunday.

We attend a church that is extraordinarily worshipful. Even as one walks into the sanctuary, one senses God's holiness and nearness in a way that is palpable. As often happens in worship, once I began to focus my attention on the Lord, everything that seemed so irritating before now seemed silly and trivial by comparison. Towards the end of the service, the congregation was seated and we began singing the hymn "Amazing Grace." I have sung it a thousand times. But how does one describe a moment of transcendence? As we were singing, we suddenly became aware of the presence of the Lord in a special way. This Presence was so unmistakable and so powerful that something occurred, something I had never seen happen in any church that I have attended. Without any direction, everyone spontaneously and in unison rose out of their seats. We simply could do nothing less. God was with us, and we all had to stand to our feet and sing as we had never sung in our lives. I was in tears. Both of my children looked at me with marvel and awe, and Elizabeth said, "Oh, Mommy, you can almost *see* Jesus!" Worship fortifies our faith and our hope and helps us to reflect on what God is doing in our lives.

As marvelous as these experiences are, and as grateful as we are when they do come, we cannot be dependent upon such mountaintop moments to sustain our hope and bolster our faith. But there is another stimulus to hope that can be a part of our lives—ministry and service to other people. We need to have the eyes to see whom God is bringing into our lives on a daily basis for ministry opportunities.

Until recently, Anita (not her real name) came to clean my house. She had suffered a great deal in life, and had been born with complete paralysis on one side of her face—something that frightened my children at first. After she cleaned, we would often talk in my kitchen, and then we would pray together. Anita was pregnant, already had two little children at home, and was trying to make ends meet. One Wednesday she arrived when I was facing enormous deadlines. I had several chapters due to my editor by Friday. Both of my children had school science projects that were also due on Friday. I had a major lecture I had to prepare by the following week. Besides all this, we had invited the family next door (who had expressed interest in our faith) to come over for dinner on Saturday. I felt rattled.

To my surprise, Anita walked in that day carrying an infant in a baby basket. She said she was baby-sitting him and she hoped I wouldn't mind. The baby started crying as soon as she started working; it was clear that her cleaning would take twice the time it normally did. I muttered under my breath, "Why did it have to be today?" I love babies. I just didn't want to love a baby that day!

While Anita was cleaning, she popped her head in to my office and said, "Becky, I need to confess why I really brought the baby. His parents don't go to church and they don't believe in God. They aren't even planning to do a baptism. Becky, I'm afraid this baby will never hear about God and might go to hell if he's not baptized. Anyway, I brought him here hoping you could baptize him before I leave. Would you, please?"

I could not believe it. Here I was, worried that my house might not get cleaned and that I might not get a few things accomplished, while Anita had compassion for the soul of a little baby. I felt both ashamed of myself and yet profoundly moved. God was doing something right before my eyes. I told her that I was not ordained and that I did not really "do" baptisms. But I suggested that once my children came home from school, we could have a prayer service for the baby and for the baby she was carrying. She agreed.

Once they arrived, we all gathered in the living room. I asked my children to pray God's blessing on the baby in the basket. Then we turned to pray for Anita's baby. Some of the prayers were amusing, like the very energetic prayer of my son: "Oh God, *please* make the baby a boy! Help him be good at basketball." As we prayed for the babies seen and unseen, asking God to bless and nurture and protect them and to lead them to himself, we heard Anita weeping. Afterwards, she told us that in her whole life she had never experienced three people praying for her at the same time. She thanked the kids through tears and sobs. After she left, both of my children said they never realized before how beautiful Anita was! They talked about the experience for weeks. Hope is strengthened when we realize what God is doing right before our eyes.

Another source of increased hope is when we see a person's life literally changed by an encounter with Christ. I had a wonderful collegiate baby-sitter, whom I will call Sally. Sally was like part of the family. One afternoon each week she would come to help me with the children so I could get extra things done. Then she'd stay for a home-cooked meal, and afterwards we would talk about issues she faced as a Christian on campus. Her faith and vitality were a wonderful witness to my own children. But Sally's questions at the dinner table became noticeably more intense when she started seriously dating a young man she described as a religious skeptic.

She had been raised in a solid Christian family, and she had little exposure to the world of religious skepticism. Suddenly Sally was having to answer tough questions about the faith, questions she had never thought through before. Her boyfriend's background and lifestyle had been as irreligious as hers had been religious. Sally was unable to answer many of his questions, and so she riddled me with some of the ones he asked her. It was sometimes amusing to hear my children chime in with their answers on how to handle certain difficult questions. I began to recognize that God was not only at work in this man's life, but he was using this experience in my children's lives as well. I noticed, for example, that what dominated their prayers at bedtime was a heartfelt concern that Sally's boyfriend come to know the Lord.

Once I had to be away to speak at a weekend conference. Sally and I were discussing the details for the weekend, when she asked if Tom, her boyfriend, could take her and the kids out for a pizza on Friday night. To my surprise, my then eight-year-old son David piped up and said, "Oh, Mom, this is *perfect*. I've really been thinking about this. Mom, I know a *lot* about God, and I thought if Tom had any questions he could ask me. And I bet he has never seen a guy pray before. So I will thank Jesus for the pizza when it comes to the table, just so he knows that guys can pray too. It's a 'guy thing,' Mom." When I returned after the weekend, Sally told me that that was exactly what happened. She was as moved as I was by their sensitivity and concern for Tom. And Tom was *floored* to hear a little guy pray over pizza!

Week after week we prayed for Tom and got updates from Sally. Then one night Sally came rushing into our home absolutely ecstatic because Tom had come to know Christ personally and had turned his life over to God. So serious was he about his commitment to Christ that he left campus the next day to go home to visit his grandmother and tell her about Christ. He was certain she had never heard the Gospel.

The effect this had on my children was incredible. We had been "in" on what God had done in this man's life from the beginning. We felt we were part of a spiritual birth! The kids saw firsthand how empty a person's life is without God. They saw that a skeptic can have a tender heart and an openness to God. They learned that when they see certain habits of a lifestyle that do not reflect God's standards, our job is to pray for the person and not judge. They saw how God answers prayers. Most of all, they saw a life change right before their eyes. When we last saw Tom, I overheard David telling him, "And you know what else? When you die, you go to heaven *just like that*. It's so cool!"

Seeing people turn to Christ as Lord and Savior can bolster our hope as almost nothing else can. And when we invite our children to participate in the process, the dividends are enormous! As Christians we have every reason for hope because of what God has done in the past and what he is doing right now on planet Earth. We cannot always see what God is doing, but sometimes he lets us see very clearly indeed.

Considering the Future

Finally, our hope can be increased when we anticipate what God will do in the future. We can dare to expect blessings that are not now seen because we are promised that "no eye has seen, no ear has heard, no mind has conceived what God has prepared for those who love him." (1 Cor. 2:9) Our hope is not based on the belief that God will spare us all trials. As John Stott so succinctly puts in his book *Romans*, "Christian people are not guaranteed immunity to temptation, tribulation, or tragedy, but we are promised victory over them. God's pledge is not that suffering will never afflict us, but that it will never separate us from his love."

Our hope is not based on our positive personality, or our love for God, which can be fickle and faltering, but in his love for us, which is faithful and steadfast. The apostle Paul speaks to our reason for hope best of all: "Who shall separate us from the love of Christ? Shall trouble or hardship or persecution or famine or nakedness or danger or sword? . . . No, in all these things we are more than conquerors, through him who loved us. For I am convinced that neither death nor life, neither angels nor demons, neither the present nor the future, nor any powers, neither height nor depth, nor anything else in all creation, will be able to separate us from the love of God that is in Christ Jesus our Lord." (Rom. 8:35, 37-38)

What sustains us in the midst of the sufferings and trials and temptations that we experience is the hope of glory. Our hope in Christ isn't limited to this world only (1 Cor. 15:19). To be a true disciple of Christ is to carry the hope of finally sharing in his glory (Eph. 1:18), of seeing God face-to-face, and having the final traces of human sin eradicated.

LIVING WITH HOPE

Christians therefore are people of hope and not despair. We know that God had the first word and will also have the last. We know that God will take our difficulties and weave them into purposes we cannot as yet see. And when he is done, the day will be more glorious for our having gone through the difficulties.

Hope enables us to push through to the end, and to suffer, if we are called to suffer, because we know there is in store for us the crown of righteousness (2 Tim. 4:8). We know if we will only trust God and wait, and never lose heart, the song we sing one day will be one of victory. For those who have put their trust in Christ, death is when faith becomes sight and hope becomes fulfillment, and our whole beings are united with the God we love. Joy of all joys, all that we long for will be ours, for we will be his.

QUESTIONS AND REFLECTIONS

1. "How can you be sure that Jesus won't let you slip through his fingers?" someone once asked Corrie ten Boom. "Because I am one of his fingers!" answered Corrie. What has helped you feel assured of God's unswerving love for you in a time of despair?

2. Paul reminds us that we can never be "one up" on God when it comes to suffering. "You were bought with a price." Hebrews 4:15 says, "For we do not have a high priest who is unable to sympathize with our weaknesses, but we have one who has been tempted in every way, just as we are—yet without sin." How does reflecting on Christ's suffering and his identification with our humanity help you?

3. What experiences have you had that increased your hope in God?

4. What has helped you to cling to hope in a time of despair? Considering God's faithfulness to you in the past, seeing the present evidence of God's work in your life, or in the life of another? Anticipating God's faithfulness in regard to the future? Why did this help you?

5. The author said that seeing someone come to Christian faith is a great faith boost. Are there ways your family could be a witness to a seeker?

6. Which heroes of faith have been an inspiration to you and given you hope? What about them encouraged you?

CONCLUSION

In one of C. S. Lewis's novels *The Great Divorce,* a bus brings a load of sightseers from hell on an excursion to heaven. Among the visitors is a man who had adopted a false persona during his lifetime, represented by a giant figure wearing a collar. Attached to the collar is a chain held in the hands of a dwarf. This tiny individual is all that is left of Frank Smith's real self. When he was alive, Frank had lived for himself. Herein is the essence of sin—declaring one's independence from God.

Now in the blinding light of heaven, the real Frank still keeps shrinking—every time he chooses illusion rather than reality. The last time we see him, he is as small as an insect crawling up the chain. Then he disappears altogether.

C. S. Lewis says that sin makes a person an "unman" because it destroys one's humanity. Sin, according to Lewis, makes the self (as God created it to be) fade so that people become shadows of their true selves. It robs us of what makes us whole and vital and real. This is exactly what happened to King Saul. He seemed to shrink spiritually with each sin he committed. By the end of his life, he had so faded from being the man we initially knew that he almost seemed like a pathetic vapor. He was a shell of the person he was created to be. Saul shows us firsthand what faithless fear, envy, hate, willful rebellion, anger, despair, and pride can do to the human spirit.

The final scene in this drama of Saul's disintegrating soul opens when the Philistine army launched yet another attack on the nation of Israel, just as Samuel had predicted. Only this time there would be no glorious victory as David had over Goliath.

First, all of Saul's sons died in battle, including Jonathan. Next the Philistine archers shot Saul and badly wounded him. Saul turned immediately to his armor-bearer and asked if he would kill him with his sword. He preferred a mercy-killing from a fellow Israelite, rather than humiliation and torture at the hands of the Philistines. But Saul's armor-bearer refused to do it out of fear.

So Saul chose the other option—without any words or explanation, he killed himself by falling on his own sword. For so long Saul had relied on his weapons to seek destruction. Now he used his very own weapon to destroy himself. "He who lives by the sword shall die by the sword." The narrator draws this summary: "So Saul and his three sons and his armor-bearer and all his men died together that same day." (1 Sam. 31:6) There is no glee in this statement. It is intended to state a tragedy.

However, the narrator's final commentary upon Saul's life leaves us not only with his humiliation, but also with his honoring. Long ago when Saul had first become king, he had intervened to save Jabesh-Gilead and risked his life to save its inhabitants from the Ammonites. (11:1-15) These people had not forgotten Saul's kindness and his fidelity to them, and they responded in kind. At personal risk they traveled to Jerusalem and took his body, rescuing it from humiliation so he could have a dignified and proper burial.

What can we learn from the conclusion of the career and life of this first king of Israel? First, Saul's downfall was not inevitable. Some commentators believe that Saul was fated to fail. But the text does not justify such an interpretation. Saul's downfall came from repeated rejection of his instructions from God and his stubborn refusal to admit wrong and repent. We have already examined many of Saul's sins. But was there one other sin that led to his downfall? I believe there was. Pride.

We evidence pride when we exaggerate our worth and power, feeling superior to others and above the laws of God. Pride has been recognized since ancient times as a root of cruelty and evil. Pride always puts self before God.

Pride is unique among the deadly sins in that we are frequently unaware of our arrogance, whereas we tend to know when we are angry, envious, or hateful. When our pride is pointed out to us, it is hard to recognize and even more difficult to admit. Our pride defends itself against acknowledging that we may not be as superior or righteous as we had imagined we are.

This camel-nosed attitude of pride is deadly. It causes withdrawal from others who do not take our point of view. At its worst, pride leads us to enmity against anyone who challenges our superiority, which is why pride always separates people. The proud *will not be challenged*. Pride must also be competitive, since it cannot bear to concede first place to anyone else. Pride must display its superiority, which is why self-righteousness and judgmentalism are always found in the proud.

Saul's pride drove him to a lust for power. Saul would not bow. He would not admit he was wrong. Even when those who genuinely cared for Saul confronted him with his sin, he refused to listen. He became angry, nursed his self-pity, and turned to others who would not challenge or contradict him. When Saul was presented with evidence that supported David's goodness, he would hear none of it. He wanted to believe the worst, because his own heart had been hardened by his pride and his envy of David.

Consider what Saul's prideful sin cost him. He lost the respect of others and threw away his opportunity to be king. He never became the elder statesman he should have been. He hurt countless people, and he caused the death of his family and even the temporary defeat of his country. The tragedy of unrepentant sin!

Reading Saul's life story should make us fall to our knees and ask God to reveal our hidden sins that he may forgive us! If Saul could speak from the grave, surely he would say, "Don't do what I did! Don't be so self-righteous and proud that you refuse to acknowledge the sin before your very eyes. Don't wait as I did, until you see God face to

face, and he must confront you with the sin you refused to acknowledge on earth. Why are you so obsessed with judging the sins you *think*
you see in others when your own sins cry out for cleansing and deliverance? Humble yourselves and confess now before it is too late. Learn
from my life. Don't let your sin and rebellion rob you of all the good
things God wants to give you!"

However, the fact that Saul was honored by the people of Jabesh-
Gilead tells us something important. No matter how much we have
failed in life, all of us have been created in God's image with dignity
and a potential for greatness. David, for example, always recognized
that Saul was behaving in a manner unworthy of the man he was created to be. This tells us that we cannot accurately evaluate the lives of
people in rebellion against God by looking only at their sins. The
greater sorrow is their failure to appropriate God's grace. It is the good
they could have done, the people they might have been, that is lost. We
weep for Saul in his death, not for the man he was, but for the *man he
could have been.*

Although David's response to the news of Saul's death begins in
the second book of Samuel, our curiosity forces us to take a peek in
order to see what happens.

While David was still hiding out in Ziklag, fortunately far enough
away to not be considered responsible for Saul's death, an Amalekite
came to David and told him the news of the king's death, the defeat of
Israel, and the death of Jonathan. The man was no doubt expecting a
reward for such news. But David was horrified to hear it.

A lesser man might have rejoiced at the news. A lesser man might
have been so busy with power, so bent on control and ushering in his
own political future, that grief over the significance of what had just
happened would have been the last thing on his mind. But not David.

In hearing that the king of Israel was dead, that his best friend
Jonathan was also dead, and that his own country had been defeated,
David grieved without restraint. His grief at the loss of Saul and
Jonathan and the enormous loss Israel now faced was expressed in
such profound, moving, passionate prose that we are stunned merely

by the majesty of it. "How are the mighty fallen," David began to slowly sing (2 Sam. 1:19b).

David's poetry helped the grieving Israelites look beyond the evil Saul did to the times before his paranoia and envy, before the raging and deception. And David's poetry enables us also to look beyond the things that hurt and betray, to see the greater realities, to remember the good, to recall what was best.

David was able to grieve instead of worry about whether anyone might edge him out of power because he had learned the great lesson that Saul never did. He had learned *humility*, pride's opposite. The foundation of humility is truth, and the humble person sees himself as he is, most of all, in relationship to God.

David always knew who he was before God. He knew that he was small and needy and that God was powerful and great. He knew that he came to God empty-handed, and that God had all the resources he needed. In spite of David's greatness and giftedness, he was not puffed up with a sense of his own self-importance. Even with his powerful personality, and as a man who clearly wanted the throne, David waited on God to give it to him. It took another seven years before the dream became reality and he ruled over all of Israel.

The thing God hates the most about pride is that it keeps us from knowing him. Pride looks down on others in contempt, but no one can see God except by looking up! David was always looking up. It was what made him so free, so able to celebrate, so fervent in his worship.

It seems appropriate that we leave David here at this very point, as he sings and leads the others in his song of grief. We watch him sing, forgetting about himself, forgetting for the moment what lies ahead, not consumed by ambition but by his amazing capacity to express so exquisitely the pathos of life. We leave him singing his poetry, as we have found him doing so many times when he was hurt or elated, distressed or at peace, in great pain or joy, in confusion or clarity, in praise or in sorrow.

Most of all we leave David singing his grief with honesty, with sweetness, and without apology, to the God he loves and trusts with all of his being.

LESSONS FROM THE WILDERNESS

What have we learned from being in the wilderness with David?

Permission to Be Human

David's life gives us permission to be human. He did not mind that he was dependent and needy because he knew that went with the territory of being human. He knew he was the creature and God was the Creator. Why is acknowledging the true state of our humanity so important? Because it enables us to see our need for God. It is the step that leads to faith. And it is only through faith that our character is developed best.

It is the Devil, not God, who would have us develop a false spirituality that is detached from our humanity. Which is why in C. S. Lewis's *The Screwtape Letters* the senior devil Screwtape reprimands so severely his junior devil on earth for allowing his "patient" to enjoy the simple pleasures of reading a book, and taking a walk and having tea with friends: "You allowed him two real positive pleasures. Were you so ignorant to not see the danger of this? The chief characteristic of pain and pleasure is they are unmistakably REAL and therefore give the one who feels them a touchstone of reality."

David shows us that we are never more human than when we pray. Prayer is our "mother tongue," the language of intimacy that we have been created to speak. David wasn't afraid to express his fears, doubts, anger, and pain honestly before God, because he knew the Person he was talking to. David's honesty did not drive him *from* God; it drove him *to* God. David's example gives us permission to be what we were created to be: human beings. Not angels who are only spirit, not animals, but red-blooded people capable of deep feelings, who care, who cry, who laugh, who need to love and be loved. God does not ask us to forego our humanity. Rather he helps us learn what strengthens our humanity and what destroys it. Which leads us to the next thing we have learned.

Sin Destroys Our Humanity

In this drama we have seen clearly what sin does to people. Whether it's David's sin or Saul's, we can't miss the fact that sin is deadly. Sin never enhances a person, it only destroys. Sin so robbed Saul of his dignity and power that it makes us weep. In the years when Saul murderously pursued David, forcing David to live nearly fourteen years in the wilderness, we watch Saul go from a man of promise to an empty shell of hate.

David shows us what to do when the sin is of our own doing—we confess and repent. But he also shows us what to do when we are being sinned against—we pray, we petition, and we wait.

What is so remarkable about this story, however, is that it is not a study of a thoroughly pure man versus a thoroughly evil man. The narrator's candor about David's flaws (especially in 2 Samuel) was remarkable considering that the literary conventions of that time portrayed kings almost as gods devoid of flaws.

Certainly David had a vibrant faith in God, which Saul clearly lacked. Yet the paradox of David, which is the paradox of all God's children, is this: David was neither sinless nor innocent. He was marked by failures, scars, and wounds. But he learned that the power of God could override what was weak and vulnerable in him and that God would use his very weakness and woundedness as an occasion for new life. He had only to repent and return to God. And David did, over and over again. He could be and was forgiven, and every time he was, he received the power for a new life. David understood redemption. For God delights in taking what has been broken and rusted by sin, what everyone else thought worthless, and refashioning it for his glory.

Virtue Enhances Our Humanity

But David also shows us that obedience to God is the pathway to becoming all that God intended us to be. As we watch David learn obedience by the things that he suffered, as we watch him learn to let God rule and reign over every area of his life, we discover that while he grew in faith, his godly character was being developed too. David was effective because he was obedient.

Did being a man of virtue make David stiff or boring or anemic? No, it made him irresistible! Developing God's virtues caused David to become *more* himself, not less. Once again it is Screwtape who sees this truth: "The Enemy [God] boasts, I'm afraid, honestly, that when they are wholly His, they'll be more themselves than ever."

David also shows us that the pathway to virtue is never quick. It involves developing patience and learning to wait. David knew that God hears our pain, that he cares, and that he will answer. But then he had to do what all of God's faithful must do—he waited in his trouble upon God to answer, trusting that God would bring life out of the ashes. And over and over again he discovered that "God remembers." The Lord did not forget him. He heard! He answered! He brought resolution!

That is why God is not overly impressed by human action or human resistance. Because overriding all human concerns is God's sovereign will. He is the only one who by his power can make "all things new." Newness, victory, hope are only possible with God. Because he has the power to transform and the willingness to intervene on behalf of his children.

Adversity Develops Character

David also forces us to be ruggedly realistic about the fact that life is difficult. He did not blame God for his trials, for he was too realistic about life to do that. But neither did David assume that knowing God was a passport to an easy life. Instead of holding God responsible for his difficulties, he turned to God for help—and it made all the difference in the world. David's story is a great encouragement for us as we walk through life's difficulties, for we see the fruit that adversity produced in his life.

God Is Faithful

But above all else, David's story teaches us what God is like. He listens, he hears, and he responds to our cry for help. It is the Lord who guards and keeps us. It is upon God's fidelity and on nothing else that our life and future hang. As we watch God come through for David in every kind of trouble, we know it is because David trusted in the overriding sovereignty of God.

What did David do in response to God's faithfulness? The only thing one can do: he worshiped! The whole thrust of his life was to praise the Giver—not the gifts. David continually praised God for his *power*—for he has the power to transform and the willingness to intervene on our behalf; for his *fidelity*—he remembers his promises to his children; for his *love*—he is concerned about whatever concerns us. Praise is the only proper posture for God's people, the only language appropriate for such an awesome God. David must sing! Israel must sing! And *we* must sing! For to truly know the Living God is to be a community of doxology.

Who then are the members of this doxological community? They are the faithful ones who, like David, depend upon the faithfulness of God. They know their deep need, and they know their only hope is in trusting the power and fidelity of God. They trust that a new future is possible because they know that the sovereign God overrides the pain in them and the chaos around them. The faithful know that because God listens, intervenes, and transforms, he can give them the power and will to begin again. For he promises to create newness of life out of despair. The faithful are those who refuse to rely on their own human strength, because they know that no arrogant human strength, power, or privilege can prevail against the rule of God. And so the faithful, like David, worship in glad, trusting praise. How could they do anything else?

David, who was so utterly human, was not afraid to trust God for all the seasons of his life. And even in the most difficult and painful times he trusted, submitted, and prayed. David's greatness was that he believed in the faithfulness of God regardless of his circumstances. He was able to say: "Taste and see that the Lord is good!" That is a remarkable confession for a man who was "tried by fire" for most of his life. But the great gift for the reader is that we are able to see what David sometimes couldn't see when he was in the midst of the fire. God used the trials and afflictions more than anything else to purify David's character.

THROUGH THE FIRE

In October 1971 thousands of residents lost their homes in the Oakland Bay firestorm. When they were able to return to the charred hillside that was once their neighborhood, they were stunned to see the totality of their loss. The fire had consumed *everything* in its path. As one man was sifting through the ashes searching for some memento for his only daughter, he found one small treasure: a tiny porcelain rabbit. Both father and daughter marveled that of all their possessions, this fragile piece came through the fire unscathed.

In the weeks that followed, the media reported that other fire victims had found pottery and porcelain items intact in the ashes of their homes. Why was that the case? According to writer Susan Williams, a minister appeared in his pulpit the Sunday after the fire carrying the unbroken vase that had been all he had recovered from his home.

"Do you know *why* this is still here and our house isn't?" he asked the congregation as he held up the vase. "Because *this* passed through fire once before." As the fires of the kiln give porcelain and pottery pieces the strength to survive, so too, with faith in God, our own trials can strengthen us now and in years to come.

What David demonstrated is that through the "furnace of affliction" we are given strength that carries us through the fiery trials of today. We will have more faith and more of God's character in future difficulties because we have been through the fire once before.

In this you greatly rejoice, though now for a little while you may have had to suffer grief in all kinds of trials. These have come so that your faith—of greater worth than gold, which perishes even though refined by fire—may be proved genuine and may result in praise, glory and honor when Jesus Christ is revealed.

—1 Peter 1:6-7